Eye to the Sky

A Paranormal Odyssey

Paula Thorneycroft

EcceNova
Victoria, BC

Library and Archives Canada Cataloguing in Publication

Thorneycroft, Paula, 1976-
　　Eye to the sky : a paranormal odyssey / Paula Thorneycroft.

ISBN 978-0-9780981-5-5
0-9780981-5-3

　　1. Thorneycroft, Paula, 1976-. 2. Human-alien encounters.
3. Unidentified flying objects—Sightings and encounters. I. Title.

BF2050.T46 2006   001.942   C2006-905336-7

Cover images: Still #2455 (*left*) contrast slightly increased and (*right*) inverted to reveal Grey-like head © Paula Thorneycroft

This work is dedicated with Great Love and much Thanks to; my cosmic family (in its entirety), to all those who have experienced phenomena (paranormal or otherworldly) and born the consequences from those who have not and to all the wonderful Beings who have guided me gently along this path with special mention to the Juvenile who led me to the understanding that we are more alike than different.

D.D., Q.M., P.T., D.M., T.R. & J.T., you are my inspiration, my support, and my superheroes; I could not have done this without you. May the truth set us free to realize the true potential of our future. My love and thanks to all, Paula

Contents

Foreword

by Janet Tyson, MA
Editor, EcceNova

The story behind the acquisition of this manuscript and the discovery of the amazing images captured on video is an intriguing tale in its own right.

On March 13, 2006, Paula Thorneycroft e-mailed EcceNova, offering her story for submission. She explained that for many years she had been witness to and had been in contact with various extraterrestrial beings, and had recently felt the urge to place her memories and "evidence" in the public record.

That very week, as Editor of EcceNova, I had begun to consider formally refining our niche to non-fiction works pertaining *only* to the paranormal. Several factors were steering us in that direction, but I hadn't quite made up my mind.

EcceNova did not receive Paula's e-mail; it remained in cyber-limbo, inexplicably, for several weeks.

Meanwhile, unbeknownst to Paula, her computer had been hacked into on that very day, March 13. Many of her files had been scanned and several copied. This was to be the first of several such attempts over the coming weeks to obtain what might have been deemed sensitive material.

On July 1, 2006, Paula had two major UFO sightings, which she caught on film. (I will describe the footage in a moment.)

As anyone who has read my own testimony will know, I "hear messages" at night; it's just one of the media through which I seem to receive information. I therefore heeded a series of nocturnal messages that persisted over several nights. The message was for me to investigate our server for lost "webmail." I had never before considered this and wasn't even sure what "webmail" was; I thought it was an e-mail service distinct from one's regular or website-linked e-mail. I was therefore a little confused, but listened to the increasingly determined instruction. I went to our hosting server and there, almost instantly, found the link to "webmail", i.e., e-mails that, for one reason or other, had not been downloaded to our regular e-mail address.

Having discovered Paula's original submission query, I contacted her with profuse apologies, even though I had no idea why her letter had been withheld from delivery. She responded the very day, July 22, on which I had a long and fascinating discussion on the telephone with another contactee, whose story is further complicated by his previous involvement with certain black government projects. It was while I listened to his account that I determined *this* was where EcceNova... and I... belonged. I made my mind up then and there. It was in that very moment, without a hint of exaggeration, that Paula's new e-mail arrived, telling me about her sighting, the footage, and that she was keen to send the package to me. It was a strange day but the effects of it did not end there...

For a week afterward, I had a song rattling around in my brain that was getting louder and louder. I had no idea why, as I hadn't heard it for at least twenty years or more. It was haunting me. Then, through a series of links, instigated by yet another UFO witness, I stumbled upon The Disclosure Project, run by Dr. Greer. I searched Google for the video of their 2001 Media conference and, to my amazement, the very first speaker quoted (and sang) lines from the very song that was by now burned into my synapses: "The Impossible Dream" from *The Man of La Mancha*. Of all things! I took this as a sign that EcceNova's path was unfolding as it should. When I told my telephone friend about this, he told me that was also *his* morale-boosting song, and that he played it almost every day to keep himself strong and focused! I must have picked up on it, psychically, from him, he suggested. Either way, I felt this new purpose for EcceNova was being gently honed by forces beyond mere whim or fancy!

So, while Paula prepared to send me her manuscript and some stills from her footage, I wrote out a News Release telling the world of EcceNova's new stand for Disclosure, and of my "coming out of the closet" as a contactee.

On August 8, I found myself looking at a strange set of stills from Paula's video. I was eager to see if we had something ground breaking on our hands. Many of the images were of lights – beautiful, yes, but lights. A few were strange, indeed, but on first glance, I couldn't determine *what* I was looking at. Over the next three nights, I began to receive another persistent and puzzling nocturnal message: "Look at the negative."

Now, all this time, I had been psyching myself up to think positively. Many trials and tribulations have challenged me in this publishing venture, so I was consciously aware of maintaining a positive state of mind. Why, then, was this voice telling me to look "at the *negative*"?

On the morning of August 10, 2006, I began to design the webpage for the book, reflecting on the chapter you will read soon, called "The Juvenile," where Paula describes staring a young Grey in the face. I wrote: "What would you do if you came face to face with an inquisitive, juvenile alien?" I then began to choose images to use for cover of book, which is usually one of the first elements to get up onto the webpage. Suddenly, the message "Look at the negative" made sense. I was looking at the still (known in the office as #2455) and my finger instinctively clicked the "Invert" button... a juvenile being inquisitive about the camera?! That's what I thought when I first looked at the face on the cover of this book, but as you will see in a moment, there is even more to this than meets the eye, and it gets even stranger!

In response to my Release, I was invited to speak, on August 14, on a well-known paranormal radio show, which I did, but the very next day, the recording was mysteriously made "unavailable" and has not been heard since. One of the very last things I said was that EcceNova had recently acquired a fascinating manuscript, complete with what we hoped would be pictorial "evidence" that we are not alone.

My next telephone conversations with certain prominent people in the UFO community were either tapped (distinctive sounds I have heard only once before, when undergoing my own experiences with the "abduction underground"), or scrambled. Our own computer began to receive a rapid, unprecedented increase in hacker attempts (blocked, thank goodness); EcceNova was sent e-mails bribing us with offers of all sorts of free services and promotion, in exchange for the first glimpses at the footage, which we had determined to keep under wraps until we could get an independent assessment, at least, which takes time. In fact, we received an offer for a feature film segment, from Germany, footage as yet unseen, and when we explained our desire to maintain integrity with the context of the book, which was not ready yet, the very next day Paula's computer was hit with a nasty virus originating in Germany! At one point, too, both Paula and I independently sensed we were being followed, and within a wcck of first seeing the images, the *only* two people directly involved with them came down with mysterious and serious ailments.

Conspiracy theorists might have a field day with this but

we remained focused and motivated.

... So, to the footage itself.

The first night's sighting starts off quite simply, with a flashing, white light. Having been alerted to the fact that there is more to these images than at first meets the eye ("look at the negative"), I soon realized that even these flashing lights might prove more significant if looked at another way. It is only in the *stills* that one can see the amazing variety of colours and shapes being projected during this first sequence. Vibrant blues, reds, oranges, yellows, greens, pinks, are all displayed, and while the majority of the shapes fall into a more geometric, or linear category, there are some bizarre, elongated, "ladders" and some spherical shapes, too.

When the stills began to show strange shape after strange shape, my first instinct was to assume this was some sort of encoded message. I am a natural pattern seeker, and within moments I realized these shapes were not merely random reflections of a pulsating white light. The patterns are not random; they do repeat, though I have not yet been able to analyze the film for long enough to determine the sequence. Perhaps someone will do that one day! I also believe it would be insightful to have the footage run through some sort of software that can determine the colour frequencies, as I am sure there might be valuable information here, too. The depiction of coloured lights as one medium of contact in *Close Encounters of the Third Kind* was more than insightful!

During the rapid sequencing of both vivid colours and hieroglyphic shapes, the 'craft' (for want of a better word) seems to dematerialize and rematerialize in the blink of an eye – in about six to eight frames. It goes from a strobing light, to *nothing*, then it fades back into view, transmuting from an oval-shaped, purple fog, into a semi-solid object that, at times, has the appearance of an elongated, almost skin-coloured head!

Some frames appear void of anything solid, but when you increase the contrast, a fuzzy shapeless haze appears. This phasing in and out occurs once every minute or so, almost as if the craft needs to regenerate frequently. Can it be that the light show was actually quite difficult to maintain in our dimension or atmosphere?

People often presume that those flying the UFOs wish to remain "secret," so they crack jokes about flashing lights and sirens – that is, they wonder why a craft should have lights at all. Could it not travel through space without lights?! Apart from *Close Encounters*, I can't think of any other serious reference to lights being intended for human-extraterrestrial *communication*. Can we be conditioned so easily into ignoring anomalous "lights in the sky"?

What if the lights contain messages, just like crop circles seem to? What if we have been missing vital information for lack of a) looking up, and b) recognizing that there is something *in* the lights! The hieroglyphic shapes certainly bring to mind a language, like that supposedly witnessed on the I-beam rescued from the Roswell crash.

This is basically what happens on the first night. As if that wouldn't be enough to keep ufologists busy for quite a while, decoding the shapes and the colours, the following night would bring the most amazing escalation that Paula and her companions could never have comprehended at the time. Again, only in the stills, and almost always in the inverted ("negative") format, would the reality of what was transpiring, way up in the sky above her house, become clear.

Apparently, the coolness of blue light, the longer wave

lengths and therefore decreased energy, become the preference on this subsequent evening. For several minutes the light show is almost exclusively blue, and, correspondingly, the phase transitions are less frequent. This would seem to confirm that the first night's show was far more energetic and required several more regenerating periods.

There are a few moments during both night's filming, when Paula refocuses on the window of the house, the trees, the clock, etc., to give some sort of bearing, an indication of time, and of scale. On the second night, when she does this, and then zooms in again on the object she thought she had left only for a moment, things have clearly changed. Now there is a strange, solid form hovering in the air, with a bright light behind it. She stays on it, transfixed, getting some good close-up shots.

At first glance, one would be forgiven for thinking it was a blob of silly putty! It has a strange, shiny, though not too reflective surface, in a coppery tone. When seen in the negative, however, this weird little blob looks very much like a small Grey with some sort of powerpack on its back!

Due to what seems to occur next, I would later rethink this, wondering if this 'creature' was actually a robot of some sort.

Suspend your disbelief from now on. This gets *really* weird. The Grey's head seems to become disassociated from the 'body' and the power source! In frame after frame, the round silly-putty head can be seen hovering quite independently – the inverted images confirm the same features (large, domed 'skull', large 'black' eyes, pointy chin), but it is, apparently, *disembodied*!

The head-like structure, perhaps a self-contained robotic unit (?) moves about and leaves the light source (the powerpack) behind. It then pairs up with another object of similar consistency (or perhaps this is the 'body' portion that has separated from the head?), which *also* morphs, and proceeds to do something utterly bizarre but, in a sense, highly agreeable ... it *seems* to project images of faces! Almost as if working in unison, the two objects create a series of humanoid faces, some that look childlike, some that appear to be more adult, and others that border on surreal (or alien?).

My first response was to think of the face on Mars – the now conveniently "destroyed" face on Mars. Then I thought of crop circles and again wondered if the two phenomena might be related. Perhaps these quasi-holographic projections in the sky are the next step? Are our distant visitors just beginning this phase of their interaction with humanity and thereby keeping the demonstration small and simple? Was it intended to be seen, initially, only by those already anticipating, or seeking out, contact?

The final stages of the second night's filming reveal another change. Suddenly, after zooming out then in again, there seems to be either a collection of small craft, for one rather large craft with lights at certain places over its frame. It is hard to judge. In some sequences, the object looks like a giant, dark spark plug drifting in space, but then we find the frames Paula later refers to as revealing a "film man" – a human face that appears to be watching a reel-movie. When you increase the contrast and/or invert the image, however, you see (opposite), quite distinctly, the being, now 'reconstituted' into its previous semi-humanoid shape, and seemingly returning to the light source, with something adhered to its front, this time, rather than its back.

In the original colour image can be discerned a very *mechanical*, solid structure (like an EVA module?), with some sort of footplate on which the being might stand, and a grill through which the light shines. Opposite, the greyscale version highlights the extraneous structure (three

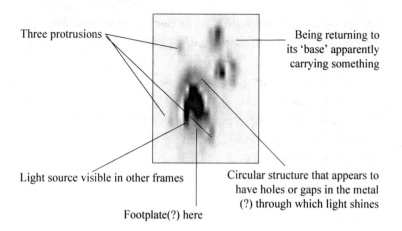

Three protrusions

Being returning to its 'base' apparently carrying something

Light source visible in other frames

Circular structure that appears to have holes or gaps in the metal (?) through which light shines

Footplate(?) here

protrusions, in a triangular shape).

The entire, bizarre object gradually moves into the distance... and that is the end of the sighting.

Now, I know we are all on different learning journeys, and some of us have insights into other realities that many other people simply cannot accept as truth – yet. I believe, however, that the time for ignorance and close-mindedness is drawing to an end. The phenomena of telepathy, lucid dreaming, precognition, clairvoyance, etc., all share one thing in common: our incredible human mind. The more we open our minds, the more we experience, comprehend, and evolve.

Paula Thorneycroft has been graced with an acute ability to tap into the universe surrounding her and to see what others have yet to learn to see. When you first realize just how far up in the sky all this was, and how small the object/being was, it boggles the mind how she knew to look where she did... until you read her story.

I don't believe in coincidences. Perhaps you won't either, from now on.

This sighting must qualify as one of the strangest, longest, and most fascinating ever recorded. We are gladly sharing the footage and stills with serious researchers and have sought independent analysis. There is nothing fake or 'set up' about it. We believe it will change many minds and help validate the experiences of others. Despite the forces at work to guard the public against such intriguing evidence, we have persisted and prevailed.

We must face our future and acknowledge that we are being visited by some pretty amazing beings.

It's time for humanity to grow up... and *welcome* them.

Post Script:

On the very day of sending this book to print, we received the endorsement from our independent assessor, Dr. Ron Milione (TAPS), confirming the authenticity and uniqueness of the footage and the extracted stills:

"Real, critical proof of trans-dimensional communication... fantastic facial images of Greys.... The most amazing observations of a UFO ever recorded on film!"

Dr. Ron Milione, Research & Development, TAPS (The Atlantic Paranormal Society) ; leading Paranormal Developer of tools used by all UFOlogists and researchers on the *Ghost Hunters* television series. For further information on Dr. Milione, see our website.

For more about Dr. Milione, visit our website.

Eye to the Sky

A Paranormal Odyssey

Introduction

_____

When I first began to experience contact with what I thought could be extraterrestrial Beings, I never knew it was just the beginning of a long journey that would lead me here, some twelve years later, to pen this account of events. It is my desire that other observers of similar phenomena might feel more inclined to come forward and share their knowledge if they read about my strange not-of-this-world encounters. I have procrastinated only insofar as one would do naturally, I like to think, when faced with exposing one's intimacy with such a topic. Even now, as I commit this testimony to paper, my family and friends are nearly oblivious of what I am about to do and say.

There are those in my immediate family who are very much aware of the phenomenon, having witnessed UFOs in the past, but even as I remarked on Christmas Day that my new camcorder would be great for recording ETs for others to see, the room fell silent for a brief, stunned moment, before conversation resumed on unrelated topics. It is not important to me whether my writing style, or indeed my character, is liked or disliked, for it is the story itself that demands your critical attention. I am beyond apologizing for having been involved in events that, sadly, we cannot, as a societal whole, acknowledge as part of our reality. I believe there are many others like me on this planet, waiting for something to change that will make what we see, experience, and are in contact with "okay" and acceptable.

The idea to write about my different experiences came to me many times, but it was not until I matured enough to fully accept my individuality and confront myself with the importance and veracity of what I was encountering, that I finally brought pen to paper. What if no one in my lifetime managed to change our narrow perception of the cosmos? I found myself wondering about the very real possibility that throughout our history great knowledge might have been lost, due to our ignorance, and it saddened me deeply that my silence could possibly be aiding (if only in a small way) the limitation of our species. Although I am but an individual, if everyone had the same conviction, imagine the changes we could make!

It was just over two years ago that I decided to really dedicate some time to writing down this story as a non-fiction, anonymous account of extraterrestrial phenomena. It did not take long for me to realize how self-defeatist this would be, for if an author cannot be held accountable for her work, how can it be accepted by others as potential 'truth'? The work would appear cowardly and fearful, the exact opposite of what my decade-long journey has come to represent. So here I am, a smile on my face and with great love in my heart. I hope you enjoy reading about my experiences and gain some understanding of these Great Beings and the plight of the individual to comprehend, learn, and evolve, regardless of established popular sociological and scientific beliefs.

The stereotypical image associated with the word "alien" is exactly why I do not feel comfortable using this term to identify the many different species that make up our cosmos. It is a term that has inspired voluminous and varied horrors created for our own entertainment, and which instantly brings to mind something that is unwelcome, unworthy, or unnatural. If more people would educate their minds in science, philosophy, and plain common sense, rather than with the perceptions promulgated via the popular media, we might just be a little more intellectually capable as a species and thereby be able to see and understand greater truths.

To date, I have not been exposed to any means of hypnotherapy or progressive dream recall. I have been in contact, briefly via e-mail, to one Canadian ufologist, back in 2004, who informed me that 99% of all abduction cases he had come across are negative. This person told me that most abductees report being raped or being forced to take part in extraterrestrial orgies! I chose to end contact with this potentially misinformed professional but I wondered if perhaps a few truly disturbed individuals might claim some type of ET involvement as a means of externalizing responsibility for their own strange fantasies. (This is my own, personal theory, so I apologize to any that may have indeed endured such atrocities.) I look forward to the time in the not too distant future when this particular ufologist can see for himself the proof of the advanced, enlightened, and benevolent species that exist beside us.

I have not, in the considerable time since my first encounter, experienced anything with these Beings that could be considered even remotely sexual. The interesting thing is that I sleep in the nude, so most times I was taken I was naked, yet all my experiences were of a more intellectual nature. The Beings in whose presence I have found myself appear to have little concern for such trivial matters as dress or sex.

This work is focused almost entirely on the various craft sightings and the live contact events I experienced between 1993, when I was 17, and 2006, at the age of 30. What is contained within these pages are my observations of what transpired during various types of waking-consciousness, from daytime viewing (alone or with multiple witnesses), and from dream memories. My story begins at First Contact and moves forward chronologically. Due to the many geographical locations and the long period of time this work spans, I was unable to contact some of the previous witnesses in time for publication, so I have changed their names and identities for the sake of privacy. All others mentioned have agreed to be named.

Regardless of how this information is accepted, I have promised myself that I shall continue to record, document, and search for the truth of our existence and evolution. What I have seen I can never forget. If this should mean that others will ostracize me, then with much love and a little sadness I accept their ignorance. As for me, in the name of science and truth, I will continue my quest.

First Contact

One morning in early March of 1993, when I was 17, I awoke just after dawn feeling incredibly peaceful, happy, and buoyant. This struck me immediately as being odd, for there was no reason (of significance) that should have caused me to feel this way.

I looked around my bedroom and thought maybe the brilliant sun against the azure sky melting away this Caribou winter was a reason to feel so good. With complete peace and relaxation filling my body, the strangest memory began to play in my mind like some haunting dream that was far too real.

What I remembered was unlike anything I had ever known. I saw a slender, golden-skinned Being (standing to my left) with hairless hands, arms, body, and head. The Being looked at me with very large, beautiful brown, blinking eyes. I was lying on a flat, narrow table in a room such as I have never seen before or since. The walls were a deep shade of pinky-peach. These strange walls seemed to emit their own glowing energy and I found them to be relaxing, comforting, and they glowed in such a way that made me think they were really alive or part of some type of larger organism. There were slight movements as the walls bent and flexed gently and slowly, much like the rhythm of breath. The only thing I can relate the walls' structural composition to is some sort of membranous tissue, as they appeared pliable and I could see some type of veining within. I lay there, calmly looking around this small (living?) room, so small I could not see the floor from where I was lying. I never thought about trying to move, get up, or get away. I was just completely content to lie there, feeling tranquil and in awe of this luminous Being and amazing place.

There was a spot a little to my left but almost directly in front of me, where the wall 'bent over', leaving a doorway. There was no door and I was reminded of a camp tent made with a tarpaulin, as the strange (fleshy?) wall simply left a triangular opening in the bend of the wall. The wall in front of me was curved, creating a semicircular effect.

I could see more of these same walls, gently moving, through the opening that I estimate had to be at least five feet tall (possibly six), as I am 5' 9" and the slender Golden Being to my left appeared to be within a few inches of my own height. I became aware of the Golden Being's hands moving lightly and gently across my shoulder and over my chest, above my breasts. The feeling of focus and determination I sensed from this Being as I watched the slow, deliberate movement of its thin, golden fingers, made me feel like I was undergoing some type of scan or examination. It is important to know that at no time was I in the least concerned. Looking back, I think it is quite possible I was in some type of trancelike or drug-induced state, for my behavior was, perhaps *too* tranquil. I truly had no concern about waking to such strange surroundings or to finding such an unworldly Being with me.

The Golden Being's arms were long and slender, and jointed in the middle, like ours. This Being was illuminated; the skin was such a rich, golden, glowing colour and of such a smooth texture, that each time I think of it, I can remember seeing particles in the space around 'his' body illuminated by an inner glow and pulse of energy. It was like a halo effect, except more particular.

Its hands were also similar to ours. There was what could be called a thumb, only it was longer than a human thumb. There were three fingers, long and slender. I could not see any indication of fingernails. The Beings' hands were moving gently over the right side of my chest, fingers barely touching me, when I heard a voice that must have come from inside my head because I never saw 'his' mouth move to articulate any sounds.

"A lump? It's hard here... Cancer?"

"No, I've been working out," I thought immediately, as I visualized our family weight bench at home.

I knew then, by the voice and the energy of this Being, that it was a male, although I at no time saw any identifiable physical indication of sex. I looked up, curiously, into his brown eyes and sensed that he was smiling as he gazed back at me. I later wondered what ancient knowledge lay behind those eyes, which were entirely brown; there might have been a black pupil but I did not see one, for I was lost inside the overwhelming emotional deepness of the complete eye, and the soul within.

I sensed so much kindness, beauty, and wisdom in his huge, milk-chocolate eyes and was struck by the beautiful emanations of light that came from his glowing body and from this peaceful, soothing place. As this Being stared, smiling gently down at me, I could not help but feel a connection, a closeness, like family. The thought came to me that Beings such as this might have created us in a time so distant I could not understand, and that this was a type of 'checkup'. There was so much love for me. I watched him, transfixed in this look he was giving me. I felt something so strong and powerful, yet it would take me years to identify and understand this look. It was the way I would look and feel about my newborn son. Try as I might to dissuade myself, I cannot, for it is the same.

It was as if I had woken up here already undergoing the exam, and then when I woke up again, I was in my own bed feeling rested, relaxed, and wonderful. Slowly the content and peaceful feeling began to wear away, as this strange memory replayed itself, again and again. Physically, my body became shaky and my mind began to race.

The Golden Being, his eyes, the radiance of the strange place and the beautiful feeling I woke up with all felt so real, I was left with little doubt that the memory had been more than a dream. I felt at a loss for an immediate explanation. The longer I thought about it, the more frantic and confused I became; what was I going to say, and to whom?

The following weeks were difficult for me. The experience was so visually and emotionally fresh in my mind, that every time I thought about it I felt unable to grasp a solid understanding of what had really happened. I had never dreamt or experienced any thing like this, and I had no way to classify or categorize it (this was before the movie *Fire In The Sky*, which, 'Thank you, Jesus!', I did not see before I started to have these ET experiences), and it was this absence of solid, viable information that drove my head in circles.

I talked to my mother about the memory and true to her own inexperienced but not dismissing nature, she had little to add. Being her daughter, I desperately wanted her to explain who these Beings were and what had happened to me (though I never said as much directly). She really wanted me to believe it had only been a bad dream and I wanted to trust her, but I knew it had been more than that. Besides, I had rationalized in my own mind that if it had been just a dream, then it wasn't really a bad one but a nice one, as far as dreams go. So why then, did I still feel so nervous and worried inside?

After a couple of months I had all but forgotten the experience, except at odd times when I would find myself looking to the sky or laying awake at night; I would remember the Golden glowing Being and the room that seemed alive.

Late June found me sun-tanning one afternoon in our backyard. As I rolled over onto my back, using my novel to block the sun, I noticed light sparkling off of an object high in the sky above me.

With my naked eye all I could see was what appeared to look like a silver ball. I watched it hanging motionless in the sky for a few minutes and I wondered if this what a weather balloon looked like. No sooner had I thought this than the object took off suddenly to the south, so fast it appeared to streak a silver tail behind it, then it vanished. I was very confused by what I had just seen. My mind could only deduce that either it had been some type of military technology or it had been something else. My curiosity was now aroused and I began to pay more attention to the sky. I spotted a few more of those strange silver balls over the next few weeks but either they remained motionless for so long that I became disinterested (and then when I would look back they would be gone), or they were at such a distance from me that they were very hard to see.

Mid-July, I went swimming with my sister, Carla, and her best friend at our secret beach on the shores of the lake just down the road from our home. It was very hot, and we swam, at times engulfed in the schools of baby Kokanee, in the crystal waters until we were very tired. After our languorous swim, we lay on the beach relaxing and reading, when the reflection of sunlight glinting off of metal again caught my attention.

"Carla, do you see that silver thing in the sky out there?" I said, as I pointed out over the lake.

"What is it?" She asked.

"I don't know."

It was then that I saw two more of the same round, silver objects approaching the one already in front of us, from the north. The girls saw them too, and yelled together: "They're UFOs!"

The two silver orbs stopped in the sky close to the third. They all remained motionless for a few seconds just above the lake, before all three proceeded south, down the valley in a three-point triangular formation. The round, sometimes appearing disc-shaped, silver objects moved smoothly and left me in no doubt that they were guided by some type of intelligence (directly or indirectly).

The girls had just witnessed some type of extraterrestrial display and were ecstatic. They were so excited, making plans to tell their friends, that they did not even notice my unusually quiet demeanor. My head was racing with questions. The thought that bothered me most was why I hadn't heard reports of these objects in the vicinity before. Surely others had seen these strange balls in the sky? I watched the News that night but no comment was made about anything strange in our skies, from any of the networks. I watched again the next evening and the night after that. The weeks passed slowly, and still there was no media attention given to this other-worldly, yet so stunningly real phenomenon.

I began to see the silver objects quite frequently, during the day. I observed them whizzing across the sky and I wondered who controlled them, where they were coming from or going to, and if they knew I was watching them. I, along with numerous friends and family viewed so many of these objects over the next few months that we began to feel compelled to chase them; whenever we spotted one, we would jump in our cars and follow it as far as our country roads would allow.

There was another type of unfamiliar object that we spotted regularly at this time in my life. These were some of the smallest I have ever seen and it is important to note that we only saw these other ones at night. They appeared to be perfectly circular and round, like the silver orbs, only they were a bright, jack-o-lantern orange colour. We never got closer to them than a few hundred feet but it was obvious they could be no larger than 12-15 ft across. These craft, for want of a better word, were always a lot closer to the ground than the others and they usually appeared in pairs or groups. If you did only see one, you would rarely have to wait more then a few seconds before you were sure to see more. They were capable of accelerating rapidly and stopping suddenly and could travel in a straight line. At times, they appeared to have a bobbing, gently bouncing motion.

On our way to a friend's party, one late summer night, as we rounded a sharp corner on a deserted country road, we saw five of the orange balls hovering over a field in the distance. As we approached in our car, they took off but as we rounded every corner one or two would be waiting at the next bend in the road. We all decided to go to the party, rather than continuing to chase the orange balls but we had a good laugh a few hours later when some other friends arrived late and told us how they had been delayed because they were following some strange orange UFOs in their car.

I know on some level I must have thought that what we were seeing and doing was uncommon but, as far as I knew, I was the only one who had possibly been in direct contact. I had only spoken to my mother about the strange memory and by not telling anyone else, no one was really afraid of seeing or following them. I thought I might learn something and be able to make sense of the strange memory and things we were now seeing. Many nights went by and it seemed that every night I would see something different; every dawn you could pick them out on the horizon.

If there was a pattern to all these sightings, I could not find it. I would see the craft at all times of day or night. They just seemed to be everywhere, if I took the time to look. I was constantly amazed, for I saw so many different types of craft. I felt certain that space was as inhabited and diverse with life as our own planet. I saw many craft that looked like glowing white lights and some that had lights that changed colour; others seemed to change shape or move so fast that their light would become like a tail across the sky. Some were circular, others triangular; there were oblong ones and fatter disc-shaped ones.

On a winter night, that same year, I had the opportunity to view a beautiful light display from our living room window. It was my 16-year-old sister, Chris, who first spotted the two strange lights hovering just above the tree line, approximately three to five miles away. The glowing white orbs (looking almost exactly like regular stars, except that they were a lot brighter and larger than any other star in our northern sky) came together and when they did, huge lights came out from both sides and above and below the place in the sky where they met. They were shining so beautifully that we felt at once afraid and in awe. We called for our mother and younger sister to come and see.

This display of white glowing light appeared to be approximately 300-500 ft across, both vertically and horizontally. We were viewing these lights from miles away, so the true size of this spectacle must have been quite enormous.

I could not help but feel an intense trepidation, for I did not know what it was that we were seeing and I feared for what might happen. The lights came together and created an explosion of light so powerful and brilliant, that to this day I have seen nothing like it. I was afraid and as beautiful and gigantic as this display was, I did not want it to get larger for fear that this strange explosion would continue to grow and annihilate us all. The light, a large pulsating cross of pure, white, intensely glowing light, remained in the sky to the south for a few minutes and then disappeared. I was instantly relieved, but confused. Here I was, witnessing day in and day out things society at large did not even seem to acknowledge. Life for everyone else just seemed to be rolling along, as normal. I wondered, then, how many others like me might be scattered across the face of this globe experiencing similar things.

In the spring of 1994 (when I was 18), I was hired at a fast food place that someone bravely decided to open in our one-traffic-light Caribou town. Much to my joy, I moved in with a friend who lived only a few blocks from where I was working. I continued to see the objects in the sky but I eventually chose to give them little thought. A month went by, and I had settled into the luxury of being on my own for the first time in my life. I came home one night in early April, after closing-up around 10:30 pm. My roommate, "Glenda," looked suspiciously frazzled, as her eyes darted nervously up from her book and around the room as I came in. My intuition kicked in as I observed this odd behavior, which was very much out of character for this fun-loving mom. I asked her if she was alright, my eyes absorbing her tense features and stiff posture.

Glenda said she had something to tell me but she did not want me to think that she was crazy. I reassured her and she started to tell me about what had been happening in the house while I was at work. Glenda had been hearing sounds of

13

someone up in her room. She said it sounded as if somebody was rifling through the boxes of papers and memorabilia she had stored in her bedroom closet but every time she went to look, no one was there. She admitted she had been enduring these noises for the past two weeks, and that she had started hearing them not long after I moved in. On this particular night she had heard someone moving around in the bathroom on the third floor but she didn't bother to investigate because there was never anything there. Her hands shook slightly as she reached for her cigarettes and I knew then that she was truly afraid.

She asked if I had been hearing things too and had kept it from her so she wouldn't be worried. My bedroom was in the basement surrounded by cement walls and I had to admit honestly, I had never heard a thing. Her index finger went to her lips as she pointed upstairs. I listened and I could hear what sounded like someone pulling open a stiff cardboard box and shuffling through loose papers. We were in the dining room so Glenda's bedroom was directly above us. I rose slowly and crept across the floor and up the stairs, barely making a sound as my socked feet trod close to the wall. Glenda's door was open and I could see two boxes had clearly been disturbed, as they were opened and their contents were poking out at odd angles.

The atmosphere upstairs felt extremely heavy and even though there was only thick silence surrounding me, it felt as if someone else was here, watching. I stifled a shiver and opened the bathroom door, directly to my right. I pulled back the shower-curtain and looked into the tub. Nothing. I stopped in front of the mirror and was feeling the strangest sensation (a slow tranquil feeling). Then I heard three different bell tones (like the sound some elevators use to announce the floor). I instantly felt very sleepy and then I was instinctively afraid. With much effort I forced my legs to run from the bathroom, step after step, feeling as though I were running through water, down the stairs to the dining room where I found Glenda hunched over the table, nearly unconscious. As I touched her arm gently, I was out of breath and feeling exhausted. She opened her eyes and tried to sit up a little straighter.

"You were right," I said. "There was nothing there."

I decided to put some water on for tea and the phone rang. It was Rick, Glenda's boyfriend; I passed the phone to her and waited for the water to boil. It was not even 11:00, yet I was feeling incredibly tired. My body responded like it was moving in slow motion as I made our tea. These feelings were new to me, but I wondered if the strange noises in the house and the distinct bell tones I had heard had anything to do with all the craft we had been seeing lately, or the Being I had a memory of seeing. I did not want to tell Glenda anything about what I had seen, unless I knew for sure that these things that were happening now were related. I quietly resolved to pay much more attention to everything around me.

"I love you too," Glenda said and hung up the phone. She turned to look at me.

"He's not coming back tonight," she said quietly, betraying her fear. "They are going out for one more day, so they won't be home until tomorrow night."

Rick and Ben, brothers and our boyfriends, had left two days ago on a salmon-fishing trip up north. The phone rang again.

"That will be Ben," she said, picking up the phone. "Hello... She's right here, Ben."

I smiled and took the phone from her.

"Hello," I said.

"Hi Honey, how are you?" he asked.

"Good." I lied, just a little.

Ben told me he had a great day catching fish on the river with his younger brother and he wanted to go out again tomorrow, if I didn't mind him staying for another night.

"Of course not, have a good time." I said

We said our good-byes and I hung up. Glenda looked up from her mug of tea, her blue eyes wide open.

"Do you think it's a ghost?" she said.

"I don't know, maybe," I replied, as honestly as I could.

"I know this is stupid," she added "but I'm really freaked. Do you think you can sleep in my room tonight?"

I had to admit that I definitely was not looking forward to sleeping alone in the basement, so I agreed. We drank another pot of chamomile tea, watched the end of a movie on TV and decided to go to bed around midnight. I had a quick shower and went downstairs to change into a large black tee-shirt to sleep in. (The black tee-shirt with a large white "CK" stamped on the front actually belonged to my sister; I had washed it and left it out and upon seeing it thought would be perfect to sleep in tonight, seeing as I was not going to be alone in the room.) I climbed back up the stairs and started to cross the dark main floor.

Again, I felt this strange feeling, not so much that I was being watched as that I was not alone down here. I had to summon all my courage not run up the stairs to the third floor, like a frightened little child. I knew Glenda was a lot more afraid than she was letting on, and the last thing I wanted was to do or say anything that would further scare her. I entered her room as calmly and slowly as possible under the present circumstances. Glenda, already in bed, smiled when she saw me.

"Look at us," I said. "We're a bunch of scaredy cats without our men here."

"If you weren't here I don't think I could sleep at all

tonight," she yawned. "I'm so tired but I'm afraid whatever it is will come back."

I grabbed a paperback romance off her shelf and got in the right side of the bed.

"Don't worry," I said. "I'm going to read for awhile, so you go ahead and get some sleep."

"Okay," she replied.

Yawning again she said Good Night, rolled over, and within minutes was snoring softly. The clock to my right displayed 12:30 am. I read for an hour and by 1:30, I could barely keep my eyes open. I closed the book and placed it beside the clock on the bedside table to my right. I switched off the light and rolled onto my back.

I gazed up at the darkened ceiling, hearing Glenda sleeping soundly lulled my already tired eyes closed. As soon as my eyes shut, my head was flooded with a sound so loud and powerful it was painful. It sounded like a huge droning motor and was so loud I thought my eardrums would burst from the painful pressure being created in my head. I tried to open my eyes, but my whole body felt like it was encased in cement with my eyes sealed shut. I tried as hard as I could, but I could not open my eyes or move at all. It felt as if this loud, low sound was permeating to the very depths of my being. I was frantic inside and felt trapped underneath some unseen weight and force. It seemed a relatively short time before I was able to force my eyes open, at which instant the sound ceased. Heart pounding, breathing hard, I wiggled my toes and stared out into the darkness. I had no idea what had just happened.

Glenda was still sleeping soundly. At first, I wanted to shake her awake and make sure she wasn't trapped like I was but as I watched her I knew she was fine.

Her breath came slow and steady and she stirred once to

roll onto her side. I started to question myself and wonder what had happened. I had never felt or heard anything like that in all my remembered life. Even though the sound dispersed as soon as my eyes opened, I was really afraid now and this angered me. What was I going to do? Stay up all night? Mad at myself for being such a chicken, I made the mistake of closing my eyes.

The sound smashed into me again, like I was colliding with an invisible wall, and I was completely and instantly incapacitated. Already tired and weak from defeating this unseen force once, I did not have the strength to get my eyes open again. I have never before or since, felt or heard such a powerful vibration that it renders one's body useless. This sound was so loud I was sickened inside and I feared it would kill me.

I thought that if I could somehow move my hand, I would bump Glenda and then she would wake up and help me. I tried with every ounce of strength I possessed but I could not get a response from any of my limbs. In my mind I was becoming very frightened and frantic. I mentally kicked myself for closing my eyes again. I had let this happen. I should not have treated it so lightly and shrugged it off. The nauseous feeling filling my head, the pressure on my body, and the roar of this low (painfully vibrational) sound made me feel and truly believe I was going to die. I felt my body begin to move. I was sliding very slowly to the left. I thought, "I'll be okay, I'll hit Glenda and I'll be alright."

But I did not hit Glenda. Instead the blackness and roaring low sound were replaced by a greyness, the sound of wind, and a pulling sensation. I felt icy blasts of subzero temperature against my flesh. The greyness cleared as my eyes fluttered open. The first thing I saw was our duplex and trees about 300 ft below me, on my right side. I was cold in only my underpants and oversized tee-shirt, as it was still well below freezing at night. The first thought that came to my mind besides, "What the heck is going on?" was a small voice that was not my own that said: "You've got to slow down your breathing; you're going to be alright."

This voice was not my conscience, it was someone else's – an external voice. My body was completely limp against the pulling feeling that took me in a southeasterly direction, at about a 45-50° angle up into the night sky. I turned my head to look in front of me and I saw the Being who was dragging me up into the freezing night.

This Being was small, probably no taller than 4 feet, and very dark (almost black) coloured. Its skinny right arm was clutching my shirt in its hand as it pulled me into the sky. I tried to slow down my breathing, even though I was freezing and very frightened, as I knew I must be close to hyperventilating, but my situation was not conducive to me staying calm. I thought that if I could free my shirt from this Being's fingers, then I might somehow float back down and be alright. With both hands I worked the blackish fingers loose and felt my body begin to slow down. The Being turned back to look at me, with pitch-black, piercing eyes. Its hand shot toward me, grabbed my shirt roughly, and upward we climbed.

I immediately started trying to pry its fingers off my shirt again and while doing so, I noticed it had the strangest flesh I have ever seen. At first appearance you would think it was black but a closer look revealed that it was a mixture of black, blue, and grey pigments that, when viewed a foot or more away, appeared black with a dark silvery-blue sheen. This Being appeared to be hairless and wore no covering on its skin. I could not get its hand off my shirt and I was again becoming frantic, partly because it was about -20°C, and I was *really freaking scared* now. Something a dear friend of my mother's had told me once, came into my head. He had said, "Paula, if you ever find yourself in big trouble and don't know what to do just call on Jesus and he will help you." I was out of options right now, so this seemed as good a time as any to try it. I called out desperately with all my mind and soul, "Jesus, please help me. Please save me."

The black Being must have heard me because his head turned back quickly to look at me and then it said in what I can only describe as some type of evil leprechaun or munchkin-sounding voice, "Save you? I'm trying to help you, you..." He called me a name I cannot remember, except that it started with the letter P and (I don't know how, but I knew) that it was some ancient derogatory term used for humans. There was a brilliant flash of blinding white light, and I saw the Dark Beings' eyes open wide in shock or wonder.

I don't know exactly what happened but I was being pulled into the sky one minute by a little black extraterrestrial and then, in a flash of white light, I was sitting cross-legged on top of the covers of Glenda's bed. The digital clock radio on my right turned from 1:59 to 2:00 am. Glenda was still peaceful, sleeping deeply. I could see movements across the ceiling like shadows, the atmosphere felt heavy and I knew that the Being or Beings were still here somewhere, perhaps waiting for me to close my eyes again.

I began to pray again. I thanked God for rescuing me, for who else could it have been? I asked that he would please send some of his angels to protect me through the night. I believe I saw huge pillars of light begin to extend from the base of the bed up to the ceiling. There were five of these lights that completely surrounded Glenda's bed.

I could see the movement of vast, dark shadows outside the lights, which themselves shifted and moved, not allowing the darkness to enter this circle of safety. I was still very shaken and I stayed awake watching this strange and beautiful light show. After about 40 minutes had passed, I began to feel very sleepy and peaceful. With one last prayer to the heavens, I closed my eyes and this time fell into an uninterrupted sleep.

Morning came and around 11:00 am my eyes opened to see the bed empty. I could hear Glenda banging around in the kitchen downstairs. Still afraid from the past night's events, I got up to take a hot shower and put my thoughts in order. I decided not to tell my roommate anything about what I had seen and experienced. Glenda, a relative stranger to paranormal phenomena, had never seen a ghost, had a psychic experience, or even mentioned the words extraterrestrial and UFO. I knew it could only be destructive to our friendship if I said anything about the previous night.

I was very disturbed and scared by what had happened. What I had seen and felt seemed to be so real it left no doubt in my mind that I really had been pulled into the sky by some type of dark-skinned Being, unlike any previously known on our Earth.

For years, when I would remember that Being's skin, I would feel my body shiver and become fearful. It was like I had seen that skin somewhere before, that it had touched me or been close to me at some other time, only I couldn't and still can't remember where or when. The Dark Being was as creepy and mean as the Golden Being appeared benevolent and wise. If I had thought before that all extraterrestrials are enlightened Beings from afar, I now believed that just as with humans, there are the enlightened and the ignorant, the good and the bad. Because I had been ripped from the clutch of that strange Being, and rescued by my frantic call for help, I felt like I was somehow protected and this helped me to cope better on my own, without being too worried.

I felt like I should tell someone about this strange Being, and for the first couple of weeks after that night I thought seriously about finding a ufologist. I decided against contacting anyone because I became too afraid of what might happen to me. I was not desirous of singling myself out to be exploited or ridiculed. I reasoned that my experience was limited to the memories of the Golden One and the strange scary night with the small Dark Being. I thought it would probably be best to try and forget about them, at least for now.

Thankfully, after that night Glenda heard no more strange noises.

The Juvenile

The weeks following my experience with the alarming Dark Being were littered with odd events. I may not have experienced anymore direct contact, that I know of, during that time but I was made very much aware that someone or something wanted me to know they were still around. Two more times our duplex was overcome with the heavy atmosphere feeling and the bell tones that, when heard, made it nearly impossible to stay awake, even if it was only 2:00 in the afternoon. I became a tea connoisseur in my attempt to fight off the unwanted naps that felt as if they were thrust upon me. The fear I felt when I thought about that night and the black Being, fueled my determination to maintain as much control over my life I as possibly could. Whenever I sensed them, I would go in the opposite direction. If they wanted to try and make me fall asleep, I would stay up all night. I was afraid, so I protected myself the only way I knew how; avoidance.

A couple weeks after the experience with the Dark Being, I accompanied my mother on a visit to her friend's house in the country. Kara had moved up north from the city and enjoyed her new rural life so much that she delayed having indoor plumbing installed in her pretty A-frame cottage. We arrived at dusk and shortly, night fell. I was sitting in the living room when in front of me appeared a dark oval shape, about three inches in diameter. It came up through the floor of the living room, slowly, and stopped at a height of about four feet for a few seconds, before it continued on towards the ceiling, in a straight line. It then disappeared right before it reached the ceiling.

The shape itself was black and smoky around the edges, as if it was not quite physical. I could not see through or beyond it and it gave me the impression that 'something was within' or that 'within was somewhere else'! This odd phenomenon lasted only about a minute. As our visit with Kara ended, I found myself desiring the use of the facilities and so went out the front door to the nicest outhouse I have ever seen (complete with a fur-lined seat cover and a mini wood stove).

The night forest was alive with the sounds of crickets, frogs, and the squeaks of bats hunting. I heard my mother and Kara come out from the house and begin walking up the gravel drive. Kara was talking about how she had to tie knots in the rope she used to close her gate because her horse knew how to open it. Suddenly everything fell silent, not just the women's voices but all the sounds of the night, frogs, crickets, and bats were all hushed. My immediate reaction was fear, because I sensed that 'they' were here. It must have been close to five minutes that I stood there, inside the outhouse, too terrified to open the door and look out. At one point I heard the crunch of gravel from outside. It was rhythmic like that of someone with a short stride, walking slowly. I held my breath and prayed they would not try to open the door.

Anyone who has been to a lake and forest area in late Spring knows there is no such thing as real stillness out here, but for a few moments, there was. As quickly and distinctly as it had been silenced, the night instantly filled again with the songs of thousands of crickets and frogs. I heard the house door swing open and my mother and her friend began to walk up the driveway, again. Unable to contain myself any longer, I burst from the outhouse and caught up with them before they reached the gate. Kara started her spiel about the horse and the knots for a second time. Disapproval showed on my mother's face when I interrupted to ask if this was the second time they had walked to the gate.

"No, Paula we left a minute, maybe two, after you did" Mom said.

"Why? Did you hear someone out here?" Kara asked, sounding concerned.

"No, I just thought I heard you talking earlier."

They looked me over for a second and then disregarded my odd behavior. Once again I didn't know what had happened, but my feelings were screaming inside of me that someone else had been here. If I had been brave enough to step out of the outhouse I might have seen who or what had the ability to put the sounds of the night on "Pause."

Upon our arrival home, my mother commented on the time, which was now 11:30 pm; we had left Kara's place around 10:30, according to the clock on the wall, yet it was only a half-hour drive. Mom concluded that Kara's clock must have been wrong, so she called her, not wanting her friend to be late for an appointment she had scheduled for the next morning. Kara reported that her clock read the same as ours, 11:30. Mom was clearly confused but shrugged it off. My conscious mind was whirling.

They, the Beings, were clearly about; maybe they wanted me to know that they could find me anywhere. I was fearful but I was also happy they had chosen a more passive form of contact.

It is hard to describe but I became aware of some type of energetic connection between myself and these Beings.

25

Often, before I would see them in the sky, I would sense their presence first, then I would look around and find them, like when you feel someone watching you and then you look up and catch them. Only, it is different because their energy contains all that they are and since most of this is foreign, and much more advanced than we are, it is hard to comprehend their power and apparent omniscience. I knew then that my previous experiences were not random or mistaken, for they wanted me to see, hear, and observe them; they wanted me to know that we are connected, no matter where we go. I decided then that I would do my best have faith, be brave, and learn from what was happening.

More weeks passed and other than a small connection of time slowing, silence, and more of those weird bell tones, life was quiet. Ben asked me to move in with him. Ben's place consisted of ten acres bordered on three sides by Crown Land. The nearest neighbor was two miles down the road and town was 45 minutes away. I was a little nervous about the seclusion of this place but Ben really loved me and I knew it would hurt him if I did not allow our relationship to move forward, so I agreed to move in. Ben worked afternoon shifts and did not arrive home after work until 1:30 am (at the earliest), Monday to Friday. I wondered if this was a convenient twist of destiny, for Ben's late hours and his house's remote location would not make it hard for 'them' to contact me, unnoticed.

Ben and I had lived together nearly two weeks when one night I awoke in some kind of drugged, barely conscious state. I was standing naked in a room with Grey Beings. I saw a spark of gold and a flash of red, followed by a grey, four-fingered hand holding a sharp, silver instrument. I watched a perfect vertical line of blood appear as the Grey Being, standing in front of me, dragged a small knife-like object down the skin between my breasts, at the center of my chest. I could hear a voice repeating over and over in my head, "Remember the hand. This is real. This is really happening. Remember the hand."

My body was foreign around me and I felt trapped inside. Part of me knew I should be concerned or afraid, but I could not feel any emotion. You know the feeling when you are asked a question and your mind goes completely blank? Well that is what I felt, blankness with no concern. My body felt shut-off from me. I was looking out through my eyes as if they were windows and I was in a little room somewhere, watching quietly through them.

The room in which I found myself, onboard the ship, was very large. I was located near the bottom, left corner. The Grey Being in front of me was not much taller than my shoulders, wore no clothing, and had hairless, grey skin. I refer to him as "he" because his presence exuded maleness, unemotional, clinical. He was concerned only with the incision he was making. I scanned the brightly lit room and saw enamel or ivory-coloured walls and ceiling, two groups of two Grey Beings, and one group of three with another Being very unlike the Greys because he looked almost human. I think I might have been in a viewing room of some type because there was a large window to my right that spanned the entire length of the room. Beyond this window I could see only a misty greyness and even though I have not been on a plane since the age of two, I think we may have been in the clouds.

The Greys in this large room were either observing or communicating. At one point, I thought the two located at my 4:00 position were arguing or debating with each other, quite passionately. I could not understand what they were saying, but I enjoyed the pitchy sounds of their voices as they spoke rapidly to each other.

The Humanlike Being to my left was taller than the Greys, perhaps more than six feet tall. He looked like a man in his seventies, in prime health. His hands were like ours and his skin the same tone as a Caucasian. He was cloaked in a magnificent red robe with intricate gold embroidery. I remembered his robe; it was the first thing I saw when I came to consciousness there. A flash of red and gold like thick luxurious drapery, and then I saw the hand and heard the voice telling me to remember the hand, and that this was really happening.

I believe the voice I heard was his, and that he's the reason I was awake to observe what was happening. He would not look at me. As long as I stared he did not look into my eyes or in my direction and I understood, after awhile, that this was deliberate. His eyes were piercing blue and the hair on the top of his slightly elongated cranium was white. As I watched him, I sensed he was preoccupied with many things. Greys would enter this almost circular room from the hall located directly behind the Humanlike Being and speak to him in a deferential manner, almost apologetic. There was one Grey who approached the robed one and spoke in such a way that I thought he must be quite upset. The tall Being calmly said something that made the Grey walk away. It was like the Grey was confused or angry and the robed Being was explaining something to him, so that he could better understand.

Another male Being, like the one in red, entered the room. He appeared younger than the one in red, although he had white hair and blue eyes as well. He wore an ultraviolet, very beautiful blue robe that also had golden embroidery. The two spoke for a moment, and then left together. I must have lost consciousness then because I woke up lying naked on a narrow table.

There was Grey at my feet holding up some type of clear bag containing what looked like raw meat of some sort. There were four pieces, all the same size and shape, like that of an apple cored and quartered. I wondered what this red meat-like stuff was and why they were showing it to me. Briefly I felt fear, and then I woke up again.

This time I was doubled-over and retching violently into a conical basin attached to the floor. My vision was blurred from the tears that were streaming from my eyes and I felt very tired as my body heaved and convulsed uncontrollably. I saw two Greys standing to my right, watching me and the Grey who was assisting me, and I could feel their sadness for me having to go through this. The feelings of compassion and understanding I felt from these little Beings helped curb my fear because I felt they cared and were not intentionally trying to hurt me.

When I came to consciousness again, for the last time that night, I was lying on a low, hard bed (that seemed to be like crates that had been pushed together) in a gigantic, dimly-lit room. There was a white sheet that appeared to have been laid over part of the lower half of my naked body. It must have been an afterthought though, because it was nowhere near covering me. The walls of the room appeared to be made from steel or some other metal, except that they were a dingy golden colour in the light cast from the area directly in front of me. I saw large doors that were partly open to blackness beyond.

The ceiling of the room was so high I could not see it in the faint light. I thought that I might be in a cargo bay or a hangar of some type.

I was incredibly tired, thirsty, and cold but I could not move to cover myself. I felt as if all my muscles had been exhausted, and were far beyond use. I lay there, conscious of the pain I felt all over my entire body, and rested. My mind was racing, I could taste this strange stale air in my dry mouth and feel my heart beating. I knew I was conscious and this was not a dream. I could remember the hand cutting me but the paralyzing fatigue of my body had tired me too much and I was unable to move even my head, to see if I had really been cut. I felt vulnerable, exhausted, cold, and scared. I wondered how long I was going to be here and if they would take me home, or was I lost forever?

A juvenile Grey appeared in the opening between the two giant doors. He was small, not much over three feet, with big, dark, curious eyes. This little Being (from somewhere far away) gave me the insight and comfort I needed to protect my sanity. Something wonderful and incredible happens in the company of all Beings, whether they are good or not, that are farther advanced than we are: there is an increased sense of awareness, as if all minds are connected by their very consciousness. In this way, you can understand the thoughts and feelings of others. It was through this awareness that I learned a few things from this young juvenile Grey. He paused in the doorway, his large eyes blinking at me.

He knew that I would be here, because this is where they would leave me to rest until they took me back. I also knew that he had asked a superior Grey if he could see me. I saw the conversation in a quick, clairvoyant flash. His superior said no, and something about the seriousness of the matter.

The young Grey was disappointed and decided he knew where I was going to be, so he would just sneak in and have a little peak anyway. He projected to me that he knew who I was and that I was coming here, to this ship. He was very happy and excited, as he had never seen a human before. He did not want me to be frightened of him. He looked at me with kindness and I felt safe because of his nice, curious personality and gentle manner.

He entered the vast room (walking slowly) and stopped when he was about twelve inches from my face, directly in front of me. My throat was aching painfully and I could not summon the strength to speak or even move. His skin was much darker than the adults and shone with such a soft freshness that, had I been able to, I would have instinctively reached out to touch him. He stared into my eyes, his big dark eyes blinking, and then he leaned forward until his face was a mere inch or two away from mine. He displayed his lack of experience with humans. I became terrified inside and I could not move away or even vocalize a scream. I think he wanted some kind of reaction, other than my eyes wide with fear. He leaned back and then forward again, right into my face. I could give him nothing. He did it once more, whoosh, close up to my face, blinking and staring deep into my eyes.

He was curious and wanted to know everything about me. I felt sad because I knew I was disappointing him with my inability to say hello, or even ask his name. The small, young Grey Being leaned back again, looking me up and down all over, as if he were memorizing me and this moment. He was happy he had come to see me for himself. He turned and began to leave, stopping and looking back once more at the door. I didn't want him to go and I was sad that he had left me alone again. Even though my body was shaking on the inside, I sensed he wasn't going to hurt me and I thought that maybe he would help me. I lay there painfully, overexhausted, thinking of the little Grey, feeling sad and very alone.

I awoke in bed, scratching at a cut on my left side that turned out to be a twelve-inch V-flap incision. I stirred and rolled over, and then Ben woke and put his face right up close to mine. I saw Ben's smiling eyes for about half a nanosecond before he was replaced with the juvenile's face from the night before. Much to Ben's shock and fear I screamed, and jumped from the bed, backwards. I saw the concern on his face and I started to cry.

Even with my eyes closed, the juveniles face kept flashing in front of me. My side was itching so I was standing there naked, crying and scratching at my left side and back.

"What's wrong hon? Why did you scream? Why are you scratching?" Ben asked.

"I don't know," I said.

I remembered the grey, four-fingered hand, the little knife, and everything that led up to me lying exhausted and depleted, while the young extraterrestrial stared too close for my fragile nervous system to deal with. I could not stop shaking. I was scared, but I didn't know what to say. I scratched my side again, absentmindedly.

"It looks like you're cut. Turn around so I can see your back," Ben motioned with his finger.

I looked down and saw the three-inch incision down the center of my chest. I asked Ben if there was a cut on my back, too.

"Yes, there are two of them," he said. "Lie down on the bed, so I can get a better look.

Did something happen to you last night? Did you get up after we went to bed?"

I did not know what to say, so I tried to make light of the situation.

"It's just a scratch," I said.

"This is not a scratch, Paula. There's no way you could have done this to yourself."

There were two incisions I could not see, the twelve-inch V-flap, and a vertical incision by my shoulder (mid-torso) on my left side. Ben was poking at my back gently and then he scratched the vertical cut.

That's strange," he said

"What?" I asked, fearfully.

"It's just that these lines are exact, and there's a perfect bead of blood along the incision. The strange thing is, where you've scratched away the blood there's a perfect cut line, and it looks like these cuts happened days ago. I don't know what could have cut you so precisely without tearing your skin."

Ben turned to look at me: "What happened to you last night?"

The young Grey's sweet little face flashed through my mind. My body started to shake and tears fell from my eyes. Ben wrapped his arms around me.

"It's okay," he said. "You can tell me anything."

I told him all I could remember, from the hand and the robed Humanlike Beings to the young Grey. He held me and promised he wouldn't tell a soul. He said I was alright; he would protect me. That was the problem, I said, no one could stop them. They could just come anytime and take me.

He told me from now on he would hold me all night, and if they wanted me then they would have to take him as well. That made me smile through my tears. Ben added that he didn't think they meant me any harm because they had brought me back.

Even though he had made a good point, it would take me years to overcome the posttraumatic stress I suffered after that night. I was overly sensitive to loud sounds and bright lights for the next few days; unexpected or not, they would start my body shaking and tears rolling from my eyes. I was also terrified to be alone for any period of time, especially after the sun went down.

Two days later, Ben suggested we should go for a hike, on the Crown Land to the north of his place. We walked and talked for ten kilometers into the Caribou-Chilcotin wilderness. I jumped a few times on the path, afraid of my own dark shadow coming up behind me. The sunlight and chirping birds calmed me and as we walked, surrounded by nature, my head cleared and I began to relax. Ben said we should head back because we were going to lose the light in a few hours. He was right, for as we walked up the driveway we were in the last dregs of twilight. We had walked nearly twenty kilometers and I felt strangely hot and fatigued.

Ben touched my head, saying I had a fever and that I should lie down on the couch while he cooked us dinner. I told him I would feel better if I laid down on the bed upstairs for a while, and asked him to call me when the food was ready. I climbed the stairs to our room slowly, each step taking greater and greater effort, until at last I stood at the top stair, short of breath and feeling faint.

"What is wrong with me?" I muttered.

I entered the room slowly, as I was feeling incredibly tired. I lay down on the bed and was asleep with in seconds. I saw a strange place, all white. No walls, floors, or ceilings, just endless peace and white light. In the midst of this light appeared a beautiful black man, wearing a black shirt and tie, and a white suit jacket and pants. He was singing to me, and it made me feel happy. I remember thinking this was odd but it was like he wanted me to smile and be happy, so I relaxed and began to really enjoy his performance, as he was actually a very good singer! I awoke naked and shivering. The blankets were off to the side and Ben was holding me.

"He was singing," I said, still not fully coherent.

"Who was singing?" Ben asked, opening his eyes.

"A black man, in a white suit."

"You must have been dreaming," he said.

"It seemed so real. Why am I naked?" I asked.

"You didn't answer me when I called you for dinner, so I came to see if you were alright. I couldn't get you to wake up and you felt so hot that I took the blankets and your clothes off and just held you. How do you feel?"

"I feel tired, but better."

"You should come downstairs and eat, so you can get your strength back," he said.

I rolled over and started to dress myself. My body was sticky with sweat from the fever.

"I think I should get cleaned up before I eat."

Ben, clad in his jeans, jumped up and said he would run me a bath and heat the dinner.

"Are you sure you're alright?" he asked. I smiled.

"Yeah, I think so," I said.

He left and then I heard the bath water running. I looked down at the incision between my breasts and wondered why I had seen the black man singing to me in the white light, and if he was from Heaven? Did that mean I had been close to death? My limbs aching, I stood up and felt faint for a moment. The feeling passed and I made my way down the stairs, with nearly as much effort as it took to climb them. It took the rest of my failing strength to stop the downward momentum from buckling my knees. I heard the water shut off as I stopped at the bathroom door to catch my breath. Ben looked up at me fearfully.

"Are you sure you're okay?"

"I feel strange."

"It's probably that fever you had. You really scared me. I was going to give you 10 more minutes and if you didn't wake up I was going to pack you in the truck and take you to the hospital," he said, while helping me gently into the bath. "Relax and have a nice bath hon, I'll be in the living room if you need me."

He left the room and I laid back into the warm water. I felt surrounded by soft heat and peace. I soaked for a few minutes and then washed off. I started to feel an odd sensation in my chest, a constrictive feeling. I thought to myself, "I should get out now." I stood up and stepped out of the tub, but I couldn't get any air into my lungs. My chest was collapsing, my throat closing, my pulse pounding slowly in my ears; I took a step and heard my heart stop (at the time I thought I did). I remember thinking at that second that this must be what it feels like to have your body die on you.

Everything went black as I lost consciousness. My knees must have buckled because Ben heard me hit the floor and came running. I woke up in our easy chair, wrapped in a blanket. Ben was watching me from the couch and smiled when he saw I was awake.

"I thought I died," I said.

"So did I for a minute. You weren't breathing when I picked you up, but by the time I put you in the chair you were fine."

I started to cry, partly from the fear of what had just happened, and partly from the confusion of not knowing what was happening to me. Ben comforted me and brought me a light dinner. My head began to throb as I ate soup and toast while we watched a movie on TV. By the time we went to bed I needed to take some pain relievers for the massive headache I had developed. I awoke around six the next morning, with a migraine.

My head pounded as I quietly dressed in the dark and went downstairs to take some more pain medication. I sat in the darkness for nearly an hour, resting before Ben woke up and came down. When he saw me curled up and in the dark, he knew something was wrong.

"What is it?" he asked. "Did they come back again, last night?"

"No," I said, tears falling, "I have a really bad migraine. I think I need to go to the hospital."

By the time we arrived at the community hospital, my vision was completely blurred, with no definition. Ben helped guide me into the building, as I could not make out any objects, for all the spots I was seeing. I was injected with a new drug for migraines and when the doctor returned to check on my progress, there was nothing to report. The doctor started to take my vitals again and while holding my arm asked, "What's this?"

"What?" I asked, as I could barely see.

"It looks like a puncture mark. There are two indents side by side. It could be a spider bite, although there is no redness or swelling that would usually accompany it. Do you mind if I check for other puncture marks?" he asked.

He examined the rest of my body and found twelve more sets of puncture marks. The doctor commented again that it was unusual for there to be no swelling around the sites, as would be common for an insect bite. He nevertheless concluded that my headache was not a regular migraine but was brought on by a possible overload of spider venom. He did not draw any of my blood for testing and simply said he would send the nurse in with something for the pain.

"You'll feel better in a few days. Until then, get lots of rest and drink plenty of water. You also might want to spray your place for spiders."

My head was a throbbing, solid brick of sheer pain. I could not see well enough to do anything, and I began to wonder if I had been poisoned. At that moment I think I would have welcomed death because the excruciating pain in my brain was unbearable. Death would be a release, release from pain and fear, and I made peace with it because I thought at this moment of pain that it might be my destiny to die in this weird way.

After I died, I thought, they would do an autopsy and discover proof of Beings more advanced than us, if only evidence left by my strange cause of death!

The nurse came in with a syringe, and within a minute I felt the heaviness of the headache but not the pain. I went home, to my mother's, and slept for close to eighteen hours. When I awoke, the headache was still there, but was considerably less painful. As if my head had suffered some recent major trauma or injury, the pain lasted for the next four days.

During this time, I came to terms with the fact that I had been traumatized. I had woken up somewhere other than my own bed. I was surrounded by Beings, completely unlike any I had ever seen before. I was drugged and cut, and I could not speak or flee. All these things terrified me and my delicate, stupid, human nervous system to the point of collapse. The vivid flashbacks were the hardest for me to deal with, as they could happen anywhere, anytime. At first I could not sleep with the lights off, and when I was alone I became increasingly anxious and afraid the longer I was by myself. The posttraumatic body tremors lasted for months and my social life became nonexistent, as rarely ventured out now.

I was afraid after the epic experience at Ben's, but I also became obsessed with obtaining some physical proof of these extraterrestrial Beings. I bought a little camera and determined that I would take it everywhere with me, this way whenever I saw any phenomena that appeared to be extraterrestrial, I would be ready. Ben came one day to my mother's place, as he wanted to take me out for lunch in town and surprise me with an early birthday gift. I did not think to grab my camera as we jumped into Mom's car to drive into town. We crested the 103 Mile hill on Highway 97S and I saw an object hovering by the left side of the road, just above the tree line, about 1500 ft ahead. I called

Ben's attention to it and asked him to pull over at the rest stop, located, coincidentally, right across from where the craft was situated. Mom's old Cutlass slid to a stop in the mud and we jumped out, staring up into the sky. Hovering soundlessly about 30 ft above the Caribou forest on the right side of the Canim Lake turnoff, was the most beautiful UFO I have ever seen.

This spacecraft was so white it appeared luminescent, like a huge shiny pearl or opal. Its length must have been at least 100 ft. I could see no indication of doors or windows, wings, or engines. There appeared to be no seams on the exterior of the ship at all, as if the whole craft were made from one perfect piece. Its profile could be compared to a cigar, or sausage, with slightly downward, tapered ends. It was so large and white, just sitting there, while the traffic roared by doing 90 km or more.

At 1:00 pm the two-lane highway north was fairly busy. Cars, trucks, campers and tractor trailer units drove by, intent on their destinations. I still wonder to this day if anyone noticed us standing in the mud, in front of the Cutlass, staring awestruck into the sky. Looking at it drew us in and we were beyond words, for it was so different in material and glowing texture than anything we had ever seen. We were transfixed by the beauty of this amazing craft against the backdrop of the rushing highway and the Caribou sky.

After approximately three to four minutes, the white glowing ship (like a jewel from the heavens) began to drift, soundlessly back, until it became completely obscured by the trees. I stared after it, knowing we could not follow or see it unless it gained altitude, as we were already at the highest elevation around. I turned to my right and looked down into the little valley of our town. I felt at that moment as if a great gift had been given to me and that an amazing secret had been revealed. I knew then it had probably always been this way. Higher Beings have always been around us. I felt like this sighting was a glimpse into our past, present, and future.

The irony of our past or present was reflected by all those on the highway rushing by, too ignorant to even look up. I told myself that from that day on I would always remember to pay attention, for there is much more here than has ever been told. I thought it was possible that this ship was related to the Beings I had met a few days ago, and I felt a deep sense of gratitude for the gift of this daytime viewing. I will forever treasure this sighting as an amazing gift of knowledge and reassurance.

It would have been truly remarkable to have been able to take some pictures that day. I try not to regret the past, but to learn from it and look forward to what I will see and record in the future. Part of me wanted to devote my life right then to searching out and documenting their existence. I felt, as I still do today, that these Beings may be an important part of our forgotten or 'conveniently deleted' past, and also a clue to where we are headed to in the future.

The fear and trauma my fragile mind and body had suffered over the last two months (the Dark Being and the Greys) would prove to hinder my progress. I am still very much interested in the effects that the unknown has on we timid humans. I would determine my mental, emotional, and physical strength as average, though some may say my strengths are above average. Although I had accepted and even embraced the contact, I was repeatedly amazed at the fear with which my body reacted every time they were near. I was continually disappointed in the coming years by my own weakness and fear. Growth is definitely not always quick and easy; maybe that's why evolution can sometimes be so very slow. I am very thankful however, for the love and patience that the universe has shown to me.

Oceans of Knowledge

I turned 19 and, at the request of my mother, headed off to University the following fall. I moved 400 miles away to a south coast island city and there I studied, and was studied, for the next two years. I first moved into a two-bedroom, fourth-floor apartment and although it had recently been repainted and carpeted, I moved after my second semester because of the sagging ceiling, decay, and all-round instability of the building. During the eight months I lived there, my experiences were limited to odd times of telepathic connection and strange dreams. I spotted a few craft during those months but most were at a good distance from me and all but two were at night.

In early November of 1996, around 2:00 pm on a clear sunny day, I spotted a silver disk from the library of the University. The object was flying very fast, so it appeared to make a tail behind it, as it flew in a southeasterly direction about 200-300 ft above the ocean. It was difficult to judge the elevation, as I was standing on a hilltop and thus seemed to be higher than the craft. I watched the silver saucer whiz by and I thought, "Interesting, they are here too."

The ones I saw at night were low over the city and would sometimes give me the feeling that they followed my car. I felt so much fear whenever I felt their connection that I am sure this is why, at least for a while, the physical experiences stopped. I was to learn much about energy and the different levels of existence. I was about to be given a glimpse of the higher realm and this would help greatly to counter my fear.

The fear I wrestled with internally was not really of the paranormal, the unknown, but had to do more with my day-to-day world and how such experiences are not accepted, understood, or even tolerated in our society. I was afraid that people would find out about me; I was only twenty, and I didn't want people to think I was a nutcase or worse, have them shun me or hate me. All the stories of government cover-ups and Men In Black didn't help!

I resigned myself to work on not being afraid and to have faith in 'the universe', because it obviously had some faith in me, or it wouldn't be wasting its time showing me these things.

I have experienced and received communication from those I call Higher Beings, which include Angels, Guides, and those who have departed from our earth plane and now work with mortals to bring healing, love, and knowledge to us. While I have limited this manuscript to telling you what I have come to know with regard to the extraterrestrials, it was at this time in my life that I experienced a monumental event and began to understand how closely related all life and worlds are.

On several occasions, while living on the island, I became aware of a rocking, swaying motion, first in my apartment and later on campus. The first instance was when I had returned from school; I had just stepped in through the doorway when the whole entry began to sway. I dropped my book bag and tried to steady myself, for it felt as if I was standing on the deck of a ship being tossed by a stormy sea. The motion ended as quickly as it had begun. I was confused. I did not know if this occurrence had been my own equilibrium disrupted, or something else.

A few days later, the sensation happened again, just as I entered my apartment, only this time I managed to stagger into the kitchen and grab onto the counter, to balance myself. This time I knew it was an earthquake, for the counter swayed with the rest of the apartment. I felt both relieved and disturbed. I was happy it wasn't something wrong with me, but I was unsure and uncomfortable about the repeated tremors. The next few nights, as I lay in bed waiting for sleep to find me, I was shaken periodically by the vibration coming up from the earth and the floors below. I would listen and wait for it to be over, or get worse.

That weekend, I tuned into the local News on TV, and was happy to see there was an upcoming report on the recent plate activity. According to the geologists, this particular region (the entire island and everything in a five-mile vicinity) experienced, on average, 180-220 earth tremors a day! An earth tremor was classified as any earth movement not having a velocity of more than two on the Richter scale. The report was as intriguing as it was informative. Having been born and raised on the mainland, I had no idea that this island was prone to such a deluge of earthquakes, even if they were small. Had I known, I would not have moved there!

Sleep did not come easy that night and by the time I was exhausted enough to drift off, I felt sad and very alone.

I awoke thousands of feet high in the sky, to the west, but so the island was centered in front of me. There was a man to my left, very much larger than me, wearing such a vibrant white robe that it appeared unreal and almost electric. He was so luminous I could not look into the blinding sun that was where his face should have been. It was like we were just sitting there, thousands of feet higher than the glacier-covered peaks. His robed arms were outstretched and he held his hands toward the island below.

"Look and see," he said.

I looked down and was surprised. I could see through the

43

transparent ocean to the rocky floored bottom. The island was a large mass, complete with mountains, yet the base beneath the water was the shape of an inverted triangle. I saw the pinnacle that attached the island to the ocean floor. There were rocks and sand falling, crumbling away from the inverted peak, and I knew this was caused by the tremors. I sensed too, that all the added weight of civilization and the accompanying vibrations were not helping. While I watched through crystal waters the erosion of this pinnacle, upon which the island was balanced, I knew it would not be long until there was nothing left. I realized then that sometime in the future this island was destined to sink, at least partially.

I woke up wishing I could have spent more time in the presence of the White-Robed Being, who was too bright to look upon. I did not feel quite so sad or alone anymore. I thought the bright Being could possibly have been a guide or an angel; regardless, I felt as though someone really knew how worried I was and cared enough to communicate with me.

The experience with this Being gave me my first idea and understanding of a cosmic hierarchy. I was beginning to see how we are all on different levels of learning, yet all somehow connected. I still felt small and a relative idiot compared to the amazing Beings I had met, yet I also felt a strange sense of liberation and I found satisfaction in the feeling that I was exactly where I needed to be, learning and evolving.

The tremors continued and I was lucky to have an abundance of schoolwork to occupy my mind, so I managed to ignore most of them. I began dating James, a biological technician for the Department of Fisheries, and late the following May we decided to rent a place together. We were fortunate to find an affordable upper floor, of a house to rent that backed onto a wildlife preserve in our city. The new place was located in a busy suburban area between two malls. The driveway, a mere 20 ft long, was barely large enough to park one vehicle. A narrow, busy road lay behind the house, and the front overlooked a green space, tributary, and the backside of a small mountain.

The house was an amazing find. Upon arrival, through the often grid-locked traffic, you could turn your back and close the door on the world when you entered this house. The view was forever breathtaking, as if the entire front windows were merely a hi-tech projection of serene North American wilderness. One could only see the neighbors on both sides if you stood out on the balcony, otherwise the view from the house gave you the feeling you were the only humans for miles.

My own insecurity and unresolved issues of understanding led me not to tell James anything about what I had previously seen or experienced, with regard to the extraterrestrials. I rationalized that I had not been involved in any direct contact that I remembered, in over a year, so there was no reason for me to assume they would ever come back again. I decided that unless it was imperative to our relationship, life would most likely be easier if I left my past in the past.

James worked on environmental contracts that were given to local biologists and environmental companies by the federal Department of Fisheries and Oceans. These contracts took him to remote locations on the tops of mountains and the uninhabited west coast of the island for two weeks at a time. On his three day weekends, my classes aside, we were inseparable. We would go for hikes, fishing, and swimming during the day. It was our habit to go to a movie on a Friday or Saturday night at least twice a month, and it was on one of these nights, as we were leaving the theater, that I noticed a large, bright light low in the sky.

As we turned left, leaving the movie theater parking lot, I saw the object accelerate until it was beside us. It kept a distance of approximately 150 yards from our vehicle, but every time we stopped at a red light or slowed down, the bright object would decelerate as well. If we went right, then it did too, and when we turned left, the light followed. I lost sight of this luminous, not very large UFO by the mountain close to our home. I was nervous and excited, but I decided not to say anything to James until I had to.

A few weeks later, we were leaving the same movie theater for home. As we turned onto the street, I looked to my right, and there it was, big and bright in the city sky. It looked like a star, all light and round, but it was too large and appeared to be only a few hundred feet high. This object also followed us, as the one a few weeks earlier had.

We were only a couple of blocks from home when James said: "You're going to think this is strange, but there is a light in the sky following us. Whenever I turn, it turns and whenever I speed up or slow down it does too."

"I know," I said. "I've been watching it since we left the theater."

"Why didn't you tell me?" He asked.

"I didn't know what to say. There's a bright star following us?" I laughed as I have the tendency to do in stressful situations.

"I don't think it's very funny Paula," James said, his glance flitting from mirror to road.

"It's okay. Just ignore it."

"It's still following us."

"It's nothing to worry about, just ignore it," I insisted.

"It's not a plane, a helicopter, or a weather balloon. I can't ignore it. What if it's a UFO and something is about to happen? Or we're about to be attacked?"

"Trust me. It's nothing to get worried or upset about," I

reassured him.

He stared at me: "How do you know?"

I didn't know what to say. I had hoped I would never have to tell him and I wasn't prepared for it to happen this way. We were two corners away from our house.

"Because I do." I looked away. "Just concentrate on the road and I'll tell you everything I know when we get home."

The light disappeared behind the hill, to our right. We pulled into the driveway and without a word quickly entered the house. Once inside, having kicked off our shoes and hung-up our coats, we entered the large open-plan living, dining, and kitchen rooms and stared out the window. My eyes scanned the sky. I looked over the little mountain (to the left) and could see what appeared to be the same light. I grabbed the binoculars we kept waiting on the windowsill for the 26 species of migratory ducks and seabirds, as well as the resident beaver, heron, and turtle that frequented this murky backwater (once a fertile river leading to a small lake nearby). I was awestruck by what I saw.

The light itself was only an illuminated tip of a much larger craft. The glow from the large bullet-shaped tip reflected from the surrounding material, revealing the dark outline of an isosceles triangle. There was also another, much smaller light at the opposite end of this triangular dark mass. I passed the binoculars to James.

"Here, have a look and then we'll talk."

Viewing the object again with my naked eye, I could clearly see the super-bright light illuminating a faint triangular shadow. The contrast of the smaller light made the craft appear as an optical illusion, like you were looking at a constellation or staring into space. I thought this was a very clever way for them to disguise their ships making it easier for them to be around us. Anyone who might happen to glance this way, without the help of technology, could easily mistake this object for two stars at a vast distance from each other.

James was quite shaken by what he was seeing. I do not remember his exact words but I do know they contained a considerable amount of profanity as he came to the realization that he was seeing what is commonly referred to as an Unidentified Flying Object. He watched it for a few minutes and when he pulled the binoculars from his face, I looked for a second time.

"Shouldn't we call someone?" he asked

"No!" I said with too much emotion, admitting my fear.

I was afraid that somehow I would be singled out, that some type of secret Men in Black organization would be able to tell from my eyes that I had been in contact. Then they might turn me into some type of postpubescent guinea pig! I didn't tell James this, instead I told him everything I knew about the extraterrestrials I had encountered, but I left out any full description of my fear, as I didn't want him to be afraid, too.

I reassured him we were safe, and that I did not think they meant to cause us any harm. We talked for hours, with the lights over the mountain in front of us. I began to hear sounds, like more than one something on our roof, and I became aware of their presence in the way that anyone does who has been around them before. I felt so much energy coursing through and around me, as if this very moment was paramount in some way.

I ignored the sounds at first, knowing it would scare James, but then he said he was hearing something on the roof that sounded like small children walking.

"It's them," he said fearfully. "They're here."

"I know," I said. "I think they've been listening to us."

I knew, then, they were here to see if I had overcome my fear. I had wanted to meet them under more normal, comfortable terms, instead of some kind of tranquilized, drug-induced haze. When I would see their craft I would often think, "If only they could just show up for tea one day, like regular people, then maybe we wouldn't be so afraid of them." Well here they were, and sadly, I had to admit I was still full of fear.

"I think they want to meet us," I suggested.

"How do you know? How do you know they won't take us or kill us?" James was alarmed.

"Because I was upset at them for scaring me before, and I told them they should just show up for tea one day, like normal people."

"Normal people call."

"Well maybe that's why they followed us and waited this long. I'm going to go onto the patio. I'm tired of being afraid."

James didn't try to stop me. I felt scared enough for both of us, sliding open the patio door and stepping through. I took several steps forward and peered up at our roof. I could barely make out the silhouettes of four small dark forms. They were standing huddled together, and then they started to move towards me, down the roof, single file. The one in the lead looked a little taller than the three following him. Closer and closer he came with each small, sure step. I sensed that they were happy.

My heartbeat became thunderous inside my chest and my ears. It was becoming harder for me to breathe. I gulped in air, and willed myself not to move. The leader stopped then, and the others stood still. I couldn't see his eyes but I knew he was watching me, accessing me. I knew he must be able to sense my fear and I starting to tremble uncontrollably, right before I ran inside. I felt panicked and fearful. I ran all the way to our bedroom and James followed me.

"What is it? Were they there? Did you see them?" he asked, concerned.

"Yes. There are four of them, but I got so afraid when they were coming towards me that they stopped. You can go out and see them if you want."

He said that he had seen their ship and heard them on the roof, and that was as much as he could handle for one night. I couldn't seem to calm my nerves enough to brave going out again. The little Beings lingered on the roof for approximately half an hour before the sound of them faded into nothing. I told them telepathically that I was sorry I had chickened out when they had come all this way. I felt bad that I had let them and myself down, and I asked them if they could please give me some more time to get used to them. I didn't hear an answer then but I know now, that is exactly what they did.

James surprised me because he was genuinely happy and excited he had witnessed what he had. He easily accepted and understood everything I told him. I was relieved because I had been afraid that if I told him about all these things I had experienced and seen he might think I was too weird, or even crazy. It made me feel a lot better that the one secret I had carried alone was now shared and in such a dramatic and fulfilling way.

James went back to work eagerly anticipating his next contact and I went back to my classes with the understanding that extraterrestrials were still a part of my life, if not a direct influence on my growth and personal development.

51

Representation of
March 1994

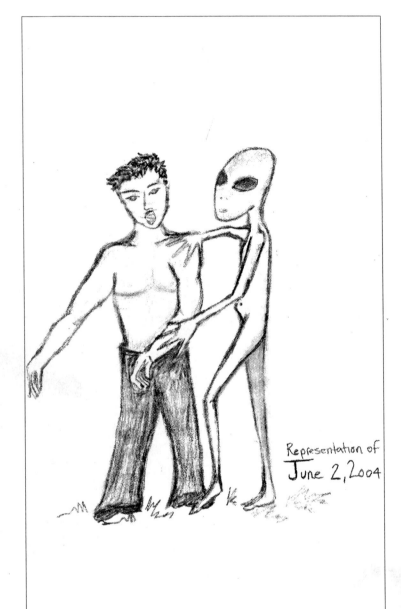

Representation of
June 2, 2004

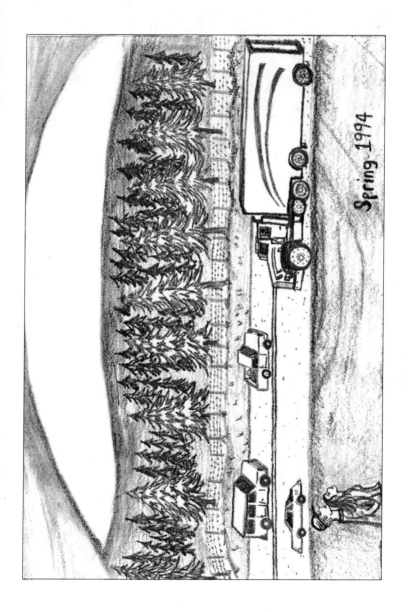

Spring 1994

55

Three "rings" left on the grass after a UFO sighting.

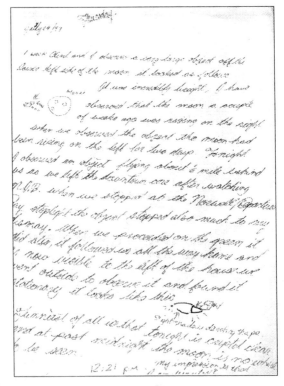

I wrote this while James was watching the ship. This was written about 20 minutes or so before we heard the Beings on the roof. The irony is that in the notes you will read that the movie we saw that night was *Men In Black*. How funny is that?

October 30, 2000, about 2:00 am: There were many dark presences in my room and above me. They were projecting great anger. I lay there and just focused on not being afraid, for they were just presences and I could see they were not physical .After about 20 minutes or so of observing, I had to use the washroom, so I got out of bed. I felt much hostility but I was determined not to turn on the light, which would have signaled fear to them. I saw myself with all the energy of our thoughts intentions and being connected to the heavens and the earth.

Record of Physical Contact

1993	1994	1994	1997	1998	2000	2004	2006
Onboard with Golden Being	In the sky with Black	Onboard with Greys and Human-type	Brown Beings on the roof	Craft in backyard / waking with dirty feet	Sleepwalking at the cottage	Dreams of different species and the Greys	Epic sightings and filming

Beings I have seen

Golden Being
Black
Greys
Humanlike
Browns
Whites
White with vents/mask
Brown Insect Being
Golden Commander
Human Hybrids (?) (MIB and others)

Types of craft

Silver disc and ball
White cigar-shape
Orange balls
Bullet light, triangular, with small orbs
Large 'invisible' daytime ship
Metallic, brown-bottom with pinkish lights
Small white orbs
Pulsating shape- and colour-changing
Starlight ships
Black triangular (funnel?) shape
Some others filmed – cannot easily describe

James and the Dogon

I was 22 and a new relationship between myself and the extraterrestrials had begun to develop. One individual started to contact me regularly, when I was at home. This Being would project thoughts and its image to me. The Being had medium-brown skin and large, dark-chocolate coloured eyes. This Brown Being did not have any hair and appeared much like the Grey Beings, except its head was more oval-shaped. Once I got over my initial reaction of fear and uncertainty, I could sense its kindness and lightheartedness and I found its presence relaxing and even playful, in an intelligent, loving way.

This Being wanted me to know that in some ways we are the same and that we are related. He didn't mean just me; he meant all humans are related to these beings from the stars. He said we are like cousins. The Brown Being wanted me to look into its face and see the similarities. I did see how our faces and eyes are the same shape and although my eyes were the same shape and colour as this Being's, mine were only about a third the size. Even my mouth was the same shape and proportion. Our lips were different, mine full and pink-toned and his seemingly nonexistent, as if the mouth were merely an opening. The friendly Brown Being projected to me the understanding that in the future all Beings will be accepted and work together and that this moment in time was just the beginning.

The extraterrestrials came back to our roof a few more

times that winter, but I was still too afraid to face them physically. I don't know what to say, except that obviously my psyche and nervous system weren't ready yet. I felt like a 140 lb failure and a bad example of our species every time my fear overwhelmed me, but the Beings did not try to push me into acceptance at any time. They would sense my fear and then wait, and when I was still too terrified and shaky to embrace the meeting, they would leave.

Spring came and James started a new government contract, alone at a remote camp on the west coast of the island. Two weeks later, he returned shaken, but excited. He told me the ETs had come to see him five nights ago, and in his own words, this is his story:

In April 1998, I was employed by the Federal Government of Canada as an Environmental Consultant at a research facility on the west coast of British Columbia, Canada. My contractual duties were to monitor and record environmental weather information from various weather stations in the area; record flow and water depths from a large west coast river, and to monitor the juvenile salmon migration to the ocean through a fish fence facility. The fish fence and camp facilities were 200 meters up a large river from the Pacific Ocean. The camp site was located in a second-growth forest, that had been logged and reforested twenty years ago.

200 miles from the nearest city and thirty miles from the closest fishing village, and human habitation, the only lifeline to the populated world was a CB marine radio. Normally, a two person crew would be collecting this data, but all the recent government cutbacks meant there was only enough salary to pay one meager wage. So I found myself working alone. I was to work a two week shift, take three days off and then return for another two weeks. I would phone out on a marine channel CB radio every two to three days for safety reasons, weather permitting.

I was living in a camp trailer that consisted of two modular homes side by side with a large hallway down the middle, joining the two. A door on each end of the large hall was the only entrance and exit. One side housed five bedrooms and the other side contained the Men's and Women's showers, washrooms and a kitchen. The stove, fridge, hot water heater and lights were propane powered. The alarm set for 5:30 am on my digital wristwatch was my only modern convenience. I chose a room with one single bed, and a large curtain-less window at the foot of the bed that looked out onto the peaceful forest. My view was of the moss-covered second-growth trees, and on a clear night I could look at the stars until I fell asleep.

One night, about half way through my shift, I had an experience that has forever changed my life and my perception of this universe. I awoke very suddenly, completely coherent and alert. I thought this was strange, as I have a hard time waking up and this was the first time in my life I had experienced immediate consciousness upon waking. I came to attention completely clear minded, staring through the window at a bright, white light. The light was so intense that I had a hard time focusing on, or looking into it.

It appeared to be just above the tree tops because I could see the illuminated trees beneath it. From the angle it was at, it engulfed me, the bed, and the lower half of the room in such a brilliant light that it almost appeared to be day time outside.

From the instant I awoke I did not feel fear, but more a feeling of amazement. I was already accepting the fact that this experience was possibly extraterrestrial-related. I couldn't figure out if they were taking me or had just put me back. I sat up in bed, so that my head and upper chest were *in the shadows. The complacency wore off instantly and I started to try and find a reason for the light to be there. Was it a full moon? Was it a helicopter shining a spotlight into my window? I listened. There was only silence.*

I lowered my head, out of the shadows, to look at it again. I was aware that while looking into the light I felt very peaceful and calming emotions, almost as if I were being hushed back to sleep. I couldn't make out a shape, just a very bright light that lit up my room, like the sun would. I resisted the peaceful, sleepy feeling and sat back up again. I started to become confused.

I realized I was all alone out here and I did not know if this was some type of biblical angelic visitation, or the makings of a bad science fiction movie. I was trying to think of what I should do, when something startled a grouse outside my window, which flew up into a tree at eye level. Fear set in. I grabbed my watch, my clothes, and my shoes and ran across the hall into the kitchen.

I looked at my watch and saw that it was almost 3:30 am. I lit the stove and started to make some coffee, thinking it would help to keep me awake. I was feeling very helpless and alone because there was no place for me to go, or to hide. I could feel a strong presence around and especially above me. My emotions were all over the place and I started to feel angry.

I spoke out loud: "If you're going to take me there is obviously nothing I can do about it, but I ask that you will allow me to ask a few questions first. I am not a cow, I am very aware. I am a thinking, feeling Being, who is capable of much love and understanding."

I began to think that only a less-evolved Being would exhibit base emotions such as anger, fear, and hatred, so I projected as much love as I could manifest, through the ceiling to the place from which the presence seemed to be emanating. A voice came into my head that was not the one I hear when I think to myself.

"What would you like to know?" the voice asked.

"I am sorry for my ignorance and I don't want to offend anyone, but as a human being I need to know if God and the Devil truly exist?"

Very quickly after I had asked my question the voice spoke loudly, in a way that was far more advanced than my manner of speaking.

"Yes, they do exist, but on a level that you humans can not even begin to fathom," the voice said.

Upon hearing this I was overcome with great emotion and began to cry. I wept for a few minutes, like I have never cried before in my life. Then as suddenly as the sadness started, it stopped. I wiped my face and asked some more questions.

"Why are we so ignorant? Why are we killing everything we need to survive, the animals, air, water, and our food sources?"

"Because there are a few evil beings in charge on this planet, who do not care about you," the voice answered.

"Why can't you help us? Or teach us how not to destroy ourselves?"

"We are not permitted to interfere, only to observe," the voice said.

I understood that this was similar to what I do with the fish-collecting data and then letting them go unharmed. They were monitoring our evolution as a species, and our physical adaptation to our changing environment.

"Is there hope for us not to destroy ourselves and the environment?" I asked.

"Yes, there is always hope."

"How many years more advanced are you than us?" I asked.

"Millions."

"Where are you from?" A star map flashed in my head. The constellation was L-shaped.

We are from a moon orbiting a planet, which orbits Sirius."

I saw a flash of a large planet with many moons around it, and an elliptical orbit.

At the time I knew nothing about astronomy, so the pictures and information that flashed into my mind were very advanced for my level of understanding. I remember feeling how very powerful this Being was. Its energy was incredibly strong and I felt very meek in its presence. I was trying really hard not feel any fear.

"Would it be possible to sit across from each other and have a conversation like equals? No matter what you look like, I will not be afraid. I would never try to hurt you, unless you try to hurt me first. I think I am advanced enough to be in your presence. I will not try to hurt you."

I heard the door at the end of the hallway unlock, and open. I heard the sound of footsteps walking down the long wood-floored hallway. As hard as I could I tried not to be afraid, but my fear of the unknown got the better of me. I started to tremble like a leaf, and I could not control it. The closer the footsteps got, the more my fear consumed me.

I wanted to jump out of the window and run away, only there was nothing but wilderness for miles all around me.

"I'm not ready, I can't do this," I called out.

I felt really bad, like I had failed. I was concentrating on trying to calm down, when I heard the door at the end of the hallway close.

"I'm sorry; I hope one day you will give me another chance." I said.

I waited for a response, but there was nothing. The minutes passed and as the sun came up, I found myself in a daydream-like state staring at the table in front of me. I felt the connection to the presence disappear and I knew they were gone. Almost two hours had passed from when I entered the kitchen until the sun came up. I know I asked more questions, but this is all I can remember. I was in a situation where I was completely alone. I could have disappeared, and no-one would have known what had happened to me.

The understanding I reached from this experience is that we are not alone, God does exist, and these Beings care enough not to want to see us destroy ourselves. After the sun came up, I still doubted what occurred during those early morning hours. I did not have any evidence that anything had happened. I looked at the calendar to see if there had been a full moon. The moon had been new, a sliver, not enough to throw the kind of light I had seen. I went outside to find the place where the grouse had been flushed from, and I found six small, child-sized footprints in the wet grass.

They were headed in the direction of my bedroom window.

I sat for hours that day trying to rationalize the nights' events. I felt like I was in shock and I had a hard time getting my work done. The most difficult part was that I had five days of my shift left to go, and I wondered if they were going to come back? They didn't.

(I feel very blessed to have had this experience, and I view it as a positive test to my character and my understanding. For many years I felt unsure why it would happen to a person, such as me. I hope whoever reads this will get some kind of understanding, but mostly that they will realize the severity of our environmental situation on this planet and embrace the idea that we all need to work together to create a better future.)

In 2004, while in a used bookstore, I felt compelled to buy a book on unexplained mysteries. While reading it, I found an article about a tribe in Africa called the Dogon, whose oral history includes the claim that an amphibious extraterrestrial species from the Sirius star system visited this tribal people, claiming to be on a mission for the benefit of humanity. The ancient Dogon, inexplicably, knew of the existence of the white dwarf star (with an elliptical orbit) now called Sirius B, which was discovered by western astronomers only in 1970! Reading this sent shivers down my spine and for the first time since the experience in 1998 I felt validated.)

I listened to James' story and I could identify with how afraid he must have been. He told me that he would really like it if I would come with him for the last part of the contract. His boss had agreed that for safety reasons it would be better if James wasn't alone out there, reasoning that if he should get hurt and be unable to get to the CB, it could be disastrous. James did not tell his employer what had really happened, but instead told him how he had slipped and sprained his ankle on the way back from the river one day (which was also true). James told his boss it had made him realize how far from help and all alone he was. They agreed that since my classes were over anyway, I was the best candidate to go, as I had a driver's license and would not require any remuneration.

I was full of nervous excitement two days later as I loaded my bags and we began the six-hour drive northwest. We drove down along the beautiful coastal highway and then turned inland. Soon we were in the mountains and after a three-hour drive along the rutted gravel logging roads, we reached the turnoff. We turned to the left and crested a small hill. For a minute we were higher than the tree line and could see how close the Pacific Ocean was. James informed me that the camp was located exactly 200 meters from the shoreline. The remnants of the old-growth forest towering above us and the sound of waves beating against the cliffs to the south made this place appear every bit as rugged and remote as it was.

We spent the next two weeks gathering environmental data from the weigh stations, identifying fish species and counting them every morning and night. The nights were uneventful, and long without a TV. We played crib or rummy and talked about the ETs. James was appreciative and excited about his experience. His view of our world had changed, and he was enjoying a renewed faith in mankind and our future. The rain forest canopy obscured most of the sky at night, plunging the area into utter darkness, unless there was a moon.

We did not observe any extraterrestrial activity during those weeks. Had it not been for the right whale that surfaced in the bay and the seven-foot-long sea otter we discovered breaking into the fish traps one morning, the trip would have been completely uneventful. James was disappointed the Beings did not return during our stay. His contract was up and he knew he was facing a layoff. I could feel the heaviness of his thoughts, as we made our way back to civilization two weeks later.

We returned to our sanctuary within the city. I was finished with my second year of studies and was mulling over the idea of whether I should stay at this school or transfer somewhere else. The tremors and small earthquakes continued, relentlessly.

I awoke airborne one morning, as our heavy antique bed was being tossed about by a quake. The bed was literally bouncing off the floor. I saw the bedroom windows rolling like waves of grass and I leapt from the bed, running. I ran on adrenalized legs into the hall and was unlocking the door and stepping through when I realized I was naked and there was nowhere to go. Thankfully, the shaking began to subside. The freight-train roar of the earth became a rumble, and then all was still.

I heard James calling for me, from the shower. He had felt as vulnerable as I had, as he was covered in soap when the quake began. We talked, but I could not ignore the panic I felt when I thought of having to endure more of these quakes in the future. I suggested that we should move, and I was happy when James agreed and said he had been thinking the same thing. I looked around at our surroundings with a new sense of knowledge. Gas lines, high voltage wires, and a million people stacked and squeezed into this small area. It was time to leave this place, for somewhere a little more relaxed and safe.

Sleepwalker

A month later, we packed everything we owned onto James' truck and a U-Haul trailer and relocated to the southern interior of the mainland, also known as the Okanagan Valley. Desperate for work, I took the first job offered to me, selling Kirby vacuums. Not what I would call a career move but it paid the rent. I worked six days a week, mostly in other cities and towns, and it was not uncommon for me to arrive home sometime after 11:00 pm.

I had been working for the company only a couple of weeks when I spotted a bright light above the company vehicle one night, in a city about two hours from our own. The light followed our vehicle, occasionally passing us but mostly it was to our right or slightly behind. As we entered our city, I lost sight of the light, until we pulled into the office parking lot. The light was already there, shining down from an altitude of approximately 500 ft. I could not make out the size or the shape of the craft with the naked eye. It was a round, bright, white light. It looked like a star, only it was too large and too close. For the next few weeks, this 'star' would follow us home from whatever city it found us in, and then it would park above us and wait.

One August evening, in 1998, I arrived home earlier than usual, at 9:30 pm. The bright light had beaten me home and was already parked high above our house. I suggested to James and his visiting friend that we should take a drive out to the hills surrounding the city, so we might get a closer look at the object. They agreed and the three of us piled into James' 4x4 truck.

The light began to move as soon as we left the driveway. James drove north, toward the hills of Gallagher's Canyon and with in minutes the light had passed us and was hovering in the distance over the bluffs, outside of Kelowna. We drove down country roads and soon we were traveling up a deactivated logging road. We lost sight of the object on our way up the mountain but spotted it again a few minutes later by a turnoff to our right. We drove up the turnoff to the crest of a hill and found we could go no further, as the road was blocked with cement barricades and a deep ditch. We could see the craft hovering above us, no closer or farther away than when we had been watching it from our home.

We decided we may as well stop here and stretch our legs before we headed back. I was wearing a bracelet with a small, solid silver heart on it, around my right wrist. The bracelet had come undone earlier in the day and James had re-tied it using his special fishing knots, which he said would never come undone. I walked in front of the truck, looking up at the bright light. I wondered why 'they' wanted me to see them, and why they seemed to want me to know that they were around more than I knew.

I pulled myself up onto the hood of James' truck.

"We are with you all the time, we are with you now," I heard a voice say.

"How do I know I am really hearing you and that you're not just a voice inside my head?" I asked, telepathically.

The bracelet fell off of my wrist then and down onto the hood of the truck. I grabbed it before it could slide to the ground. When I looked up from retrieving the bracelet, I saw a man sitting not more than 10 ft away from me on the cement barricade.

He was a young man, completely human-looking, with sparkling blue eyes and golden hair. He appeared to be no older than his mid-twenties. He wore blue jeans and a blue and white plaid shirt, partially undone, with a white shirt beneath it. I did not notice his footwear, but I thought how much he looked just like a regular person. He was smiling like he was immensely happy and about to laugh, as his mouth opened slightly. His blue eyes were twinkling with much humor and intelligence, then he was gone, and I screamed, like the girl I am.

James and his friend were at my side in seconds, concerned I might have seen a bear or cougar. They were shocked to learn my bracelet had come off. James remarked that maybe they wanted us to know they could manipulate physical objects, even on our person. The guys wanted to stay for a bit longer, but I just wanted to go home. The Being had scared me. I thought maybe he had been about to laugh because he knew how I was going to react. I felt I had failed once again, to overcome my fear of those who are different and more advanced than we are.

The light beat us back to the house, and that night, as James and I lay in bed talking about the ETs, I felt comfortable and safe. I sent out the thought to them that I welcomed these experiences as an opportunity for me to grow and become a better person. I would have to work on opening my mind to the idea of being more accepting, regardless of the lack of immediate information. I was unprepared and unknowing of what I saw, so I repeatedly fell victim to my survival instinct. I determined to remind myself that these Beings had not been threatening and that I did not need to fear them.

I had the first of a series of similar dreamlike experiences that night. In hindsight, I am 99% positive these were not ordinary dreams but actual events. I 'dreamt' I awoke in a strange, catatonic state, feeling I must go outside. I walked through the house and out the back door. I could see a small, white, circular disc-shaped craft on our back lawn. I walked towards it, down the steps, through the gate and into the back yard. I do not remember beyond walking to the rear of the ship and a door opening. Then, I saw the grass, wet with dew and my feet walking back through the gate, up the stairs, and into the house. I remember feeling concerned that someone might see me in my bed shirt, which barely covered me.

I first thought these were just strange dream fragments, until I woke up one morning about a month later, with grass, leaves, and mud in my bed. I was shocked into the realization that these nocturnal rambles were actually physical, not just mental sojourns! My dirty feet were evidence that I was leaving my house at night. Sometime after I had showered and gone to bed, while the rest of the city slept, I was waking in an altered state and leaving my house. And doing what? Hanging out with some nice Beings in their cool-looking, pearly little craft in my backyard?

Fortune or misfortune, my complete lack of superfluous funds prevented me seeking any professional help that might have revealed a more in-depth recall of information. Should there be a time in the future when science might shed some light on what took place in those early morning hours, I will gladly share any knowledge or insight with all. I accepted what was happening but I was a little nervous, as anyone who discovers they have been sleepwalking with extraterrestrials might be!

My work and life at the time were demanding every ounce of energy I possessed to make enough money to keep me afloat. I was working on 100% commission and even though I was #1 at our company's location for sales, I was forced to quit because of the physical side effects I began to suffer.

The six-day weeks, up to eighteen hours a day, had taken their toll; I lost thirty-two pounds in just over six weeks. Had I weight to lose this might have been welcome, but I was not chunky or even a little plump, so the drastic loss of weight left me looking bedraggled and unhealthy.

The long days, mandatory by the company for all entry-level staff, claimed my relationship with James. I had little time or energy left after work. I was looking but could not find another job, so when James accepted an environmental job in another city, we separated.

James kept in contact, calling every few days to check on me. He was concerned about the physical effects of my job and he wanted us to reconcile. I told him about the memories I had been waking up with, and how the other morning I had awoke with dirty feet and bits of grass and leaves in the bed. He convinced me that he should come up for the weekend and confirm for himself that I wasn't in any danger.

I was still working at the bad-career/health-choice job when I arrived home earlier than usual on a Saturday night. It was shortly past 8:30 pm, when James met me in the driveway as I jumped out of the company vehicle.

"Hey, you didn't tell me about the landing pads in the backyard."

"What landing pads?" I asked.

"There are three of them," he said.

I followed James into the backyard and there, in the fading daylight, I saw clearly three dark rings at different spots on our lawn. Living in a semiarid region with water restrictions, it is not uncommon for many lawns to be brown by the end summer, as it was now.

These rings were a deeper forest green than I have ever seen grass grow, and stood out in stark contrast to our sun-dried lawn. The rings (all three of them) appeared to be exactly the same size, all approximately 15 ft in diameter. I did not think then to measure the rings or to take a soil sample. Where the rings were there was a perfect, approximately three-inch-wide outline of darker grass: the perimeter looked like a dark green ring with dead grass within and without.

I felt a powerful surge of emotion well inside of me, for here was more 'proof'. I ran into the house and grabbed my small camera. From the hot tub deck you could clearly see all three of the dark green circles. I snapped some pictures and I was pleased after they had been developed that they turned out so well. I knew then that I hoped one day to share with others all the wonderful things and Beings that I have seen, but I also knew that without a mountain of evidence to substantiate my findings, people might not take seriously what had been happening to me.

I never had anymore memories or information come to me regarding those somnambulant nights. I was aware, though, that something had changed within me. I felt happier and more carefree than I had in years. I don't know how, without any memory, but I sensed that these Beings were caring and benevolent and that they wanted me to think of them as friends. I do. Every time I would think about them, and the dark rings in the grass, I would find myself smiling. I had the sense that what I was doing was fun and that it was okay not to worry. I still felt a bit apprehensive but I was willing and excited to see where this relationship would lead and what I might learn along the way.

The craft continued to alert me of their presence almost daily. Their bright lights would flash around our sky without a sound and then hover silently high above our house. At times I wondered if they were watching out for *me*, or were they watching others too?

Several weeks after the circles in the back lawn were discovered, James and I made a trip north to visit to some of his relatives in a neighboring city. As we were leaving town, around 2 pm, we saw the most amazing display of extraterrestrial technology that I have ever witnessed. James saw it first and immediately pulled off to the side of the busy city street. We stared up in awe at a ship at least three city blocks wide and five blocks long. We pulled over about a mile to the west of the craft, but it still appeared enormous.

The craft itself was triangular and almost transparent. It descended from the sky at a 15° angle and the outline became completely visible at the exact moment it crossed over in front of a small, grass-covered mountain. It reflected the sky and the hillside. It was like seeing some sort of a 'cloaking device' in action. The craft was traveling from southeast to northwest, at a speed of about 20-30 mph. It did not alter its course once it had descended to an elevation of about 200 ft above the city of Kelowna, over Rutland.

The entire craft was now invisible, except for the outline of the perimeter. Every surface reflected what was already there, so this ship created an optical illusion that was fantastic to see. There it was, at two in the afternoon, lazily making its way from one side of the valley to the next, in a city of 150,000 plus people. The sighting lasted for about five minutes, until we could no longer make out its enormous but increasingly indistinct outline.

I will never forget how incredible it looked when part of it was in the sky reflecting sky, and part was over the mountain reflecting the mountain. Imagine a blue sky with white stratus clouds and a mountain below. Now see in your mind the point where the mountain meets the sky and imagine a large triangular outline engulfing part of the mountain and part of the sky. The outline is superimposed over the mountain and the sky, so what you see within is a slightly hazy reflection of what is physically there in the environment. To the naked eye, the craft had the appearance of heat waves, or a mirage and we would come to refer to this as the "Day Craft." Such ingenuity! I know for a fact that the military are developing similar technologies for camouflage, so it makes me wonder where they *really* got the idea from!

We tuned in to the local News that night and we were a little disheartened when there was no mention of any unidentified aircraft. It seemed, once again, that something out of this world had gone by unnoticed, except by us. Not many nights had passed since we saw the Day Ship, when a group of young men who shared a lake side residence reported that they had seen an extremely large UFO fly across the lake and over their house, as they sat on their deck with friends. These men were deemed reputable and knowledgeable, as three out of the four worked for a major local airport. They reported that the craft was triangular in shape and was easily the size of a football field. They claimed that there were no lights, just a black triangular mass that covered part of the sky, leaving it devoid of stars, and this was how they first spotted the ship. They said that after a friend had exclaimed how part of the clear night sky was missing its stars, they had all focused their attention and then remarked that the mass of black was moving toward them. The ship flew over their house and towards the mountains. They were all excited but confused about what they had seen.

Their vivid account of the large triangular UFO dominated our airwaves for the next two days. The four witnesses were shocked and amazed and, understandably, the fourth roommate declined to make a statement, for fear of reprisals. The immense size and shape of the ship the men reported sounded eerily similar to the large invisible ship James and I had seen a few days earlier.

I am truly amazed that thousands of people from all over our planet have been reporting sightings and extraterrestrial phenomena for hundreds, if not thousands of years, yet in all this time we have failed to acquire definitive proof, or find anyone with authority to state they do exist. Much time and energy must be wasted to discredit proof and keep the public ignorant of these great Advanced Beings who visit us and monitor us (more than we know). Why do we still live in such an uninformed, close-minded society, where there is virtually no support for people such as myself?

With all the great minds that have come before us, why have we not accepted these Beings and their different levels of existence, and altered our consciousness so that we may embrace the truth and our future? I believe there are those within our societies, governments, and militaries who do know much of the truth of these matters, but are withholding the information from the public. Regardless, these more evolved Beings want all of us to know the truth about them and ourselves. This is most likely why they are in repeated contact with regular people, because some people in powerful positions here on Earth have abused their knowledge and responsibility.

Without information we cannot learn, without learning we stagnate and cease to evolve. Stagnation leads to decay and devastation, the situation many nations are and will be faced with, as a result of following the destructive path of our past. However, this is not what these Higher Beings want for us. There is much thought about our species' decline and possible annihilation and it is because of this that these higher intelligences are stepping in and desiring that we take notice of them. They are attempting to wake us from our selfish insistence on personal advancement at the cost of others and our environment. They want us to realize there is much more to life than our own ignorant, greedy ego. This was the path that destroyed those great civilizations before us and the same one that will insure our downfall now. Rest assured, this will not be allowed happen again (the Beings say). I thank the God who created this system of universes, and for the truly enlightened individuals who really care for our survival and success, even when those humans in power on our planet behave so recklessly. It is not my aim to sit in judgement of those who have abused knowledge and power; in fact, even I can think of a few good reasons why they have sustained our ignorance. I am very thankful, however, for the imminent culmination of our past, and for the emergence of a potentially bright, new future.

After about three days, we never again heard about the men who had reported the large UFO. Their sighting was like a pebble thrown into the night pond of our immediate society, causing not even a ripple, let alone change.

James and I reconciled in early December of 1998. We moved into a two-bedroom ground floor apartment and saw little of the sky at night. I was busy with my new psychic counseling job (that I got by some strange twist of fate, but that is another story) and James commuted daily to work in another city. I would see lights shining some nights over our city, on my way home from work, and occasionally there was one parked high above our apartment complex. When I would notice them, I would think, "There you are," and send them a hello, telepathically.

Beyond this simple exchange we did not have anymore direct contact, that I know of, for about six months.

In their absence, I relaxed comfortably back into life, happy for both of us to be earning good incomes and in jobs where we felt good about our work and valued. In February, 1999, my mother called to inform me that my sister, who was still living in the Caribou, had come down for a few weeks with her infant daughter. As I had only seen my niece for a few brief weeks before I moved to the Okanagan, I decided to take a couple days off of work, and seize this opportunity to visit with my little niece and sister.

Two days later, I was arriving at my mother's house about an hour and a half south of the city where James and I lived. I was having a lot of fun playing with my niece, who was in the midst of her early toddler stage. Her antics and mimicked adult behavior were executed with such exactness she was a riot to watch and interact with. James called the following evening. He asked me the standard 'how was I doing' stuff and I could tell by his strained and nervous voice that something was wrong. I answered him by asking if he was okay. He said that he wasn't and that he wanted me to return the next day, if possible.

He told me that the night I had left he been overcome by an extremely tired feeling at about 8:30 pm. He was sitting on the couch with barely enough energy to move when he heard what he thought sounded like someone going through the boxes of my journals, writing, and poetry in our spare bedroom. Of course, every time he got off the couch to see who was there, all was quiet. He said he could clearly see someone had been digging through the boxes because some of them had been moved and others were left open.

I remembered back to 1994, when I was eighteen and Glenda had told me almost the exact same story. James told me that it was happening again tonight and that is why he had called to ask if I would come back sooner, because at least together he did not feel so afraid or alone. I agreed immediately to leave the next day. I hung up the phone and told my family I had to leave because I was needed back at work.

I have talked about most of my experiences with my youngest sibling, Carla, who has a natural fearless fascination and love for life in all its forms. It was with Carla that I first coined our inside joke: "Aaaah, I feel sleepy."

I had told Carla about the many times when I received communication from or had other experiences with a Higher Entity, an extreme sleepiness would come over my entire body, complete with yawns and drooping eyes. Lulled by this trancelike state, you fall asleep very quickly. The only way to fight it is to leap up immediately and to consume a good amount of stimulant, like caffeine or sugar. If you don't fight this effect and you fall asleep, there is a good chance you might recall a bit of what is said or done, if not everything. I have received many communications from ghosts, guides, extraterrestrials, and even living humans this way, although at this time in my life I do not know how or why this is.

James was also aware of the sleepy effect and this bothered him because he had to endure it alone, while I was gone. I arrived home in the afternoon, to James' relief. That evening, shortly before 9:00 pm, we were sitting on the couch together when we both started yawning and feeling extremely tired. I suggested that we go to bed immediately and see what would happen. We fell asleep shortly, and awoke early the next morning. Neither of us could remember even a piece of a dream.

I got up to start the coffee maker for James, who is a little slower than me in the morning. On my way back from the kitchen I noticed leaves tracked across our carpet from the patio door. Anyone who lives in a big city knows that you don't leave your doors unlocked, ever, even if you live on the 25th floor, you come home and lock the door. You will unlock the door to retrieve the newspaper and then you will close and lock the door again. Even though you know the doors are locked, you will probably check them once or twice before bed. I guess we have home invasions to thank for this paranoid behavior. Our patio was locked that previous night, as it still was in the morning, yet I could clearly see a trail of leaves and wet grass tracked across the living room carpet, towards the hall that led to the bedrooms.

I bent down to get a closer look at the small trail of debris and discovered amongst the grass and leaves a strange yellow substance. Without giving it much thought, I reached down and pinched a bit between my fingers. The powder was very dry and did not form into a ball under my fingers, or even compress. It was a very bright, deep, yellow, like that of cooked egg yolk. I had read somewhere that some abductees had reported a strange yellow powder residue that was found on their clothes, or in their houses, so I grabbed an envelope, placed a good pinch of the powder inside and sealed it in a plastic bag, with the full intention of having this substance tested one day in the future. Mysteriously, the bag and its contents disappeared some time later. I have no idea what happened to it.

This was a great year for proof; first the picture of the rings on the back lawn and now this strange yellow powder. I don't think it's the "truth" but the "*proof* of the truth" that will set us free! I know that even some of my most trusted friends and relatives, who have known me my whole life and accept me as an honest, sincere, kind, and loving individual, don't believe (or perhaps don't want to) the things that I have shared with them, with respect to paranormal phenomena and potential extraterrestrial activity. This, in turn, creates a great contradiction for them, for on the one hand, they know me to be honest and truthful, but on the other, they discover an innate fear of the unknown and thus desire to reject the truth and, therefore, me.

One sure way to lose friends or weed out the weak ones is to tell them you know that extraterrestrial Beings exist because you've seen them many times with your own eyes. I probably have friends today because I have not done this too many times. I guess I can say I have learned a few valuable lessons about human behavior.

I returned to the bedroom and showed the powder to James, who decided to get up and inspect the living room for himself. He was confused about how the debris had got in here, as the patio door had been locked and showed no sign of forced entry.

"I think they probably use telekinesis to get through locks," I said

The footsteps appeared to be of a five- to six-year-old child (approximately four to five inches long). It was clear by the tracking of the leaves that whoever had left this mess had a small stride and therefore it was unlikely that they were taller than four feet. The yellow powder was spread out but there were two places where it had formed distinct piles, as if the one who had left it had stood still momentarily, allowing the powder to pool. We drank our coffees and stared at the odd remnants from the night before. After making sure I had a good sample of the powder, I vacuumed up the rest, while James was in the shower.

Baby on Board

After my discovery of the yellow powder, I felt a heightened sense of awareness and presence. I was very conscious of a powerful charging sensation of energy that seemed to be everywhere. During the nights that followed, the energy was so strong that it was very hard for me to get to sleep. I kept thinking of the grass rings and wondering if the craft were landing somewhere close by. The grass space outside our patio door was not much more than ten feet wide, beyond which was a wooden fence with a 12 ft hedge, and beyond that, the parking lot of a Jehovah's Witnesses' church.

On my way home from work one night, I stopped by the parking lot and discovered a perfect circle baked into the asphalt. This asphalt circle looked to be the same size as the rings James had discovered in our back yard last year. I believe the thoughts coming into my head that led me to be curious and look here were pprojected to my mind by the extraterrestrial Beings. Such thoughts are always about revealing them to me more fully and usually lead me to some evidence of them, or a deeper understanding. I felt like they were trying to let me know, by showing me their landing site, that they did not want to appear 'sneaky' if they didn't have to.

The heightened sense of energy persisted and I found myself thinking about all my experiences and what this culmination of events was pointing me towards. I felt that something very wonderful was happening and that they were encouraging me to be exceedingly happy and to rejoice for something, I just didn't know what.

I did not have to wait long to find out what this new empowering energy was trying to tell me. Two days later I was taking a pregnancy test. The original test and the one that followed an hour later both read positive. James was, appropriately, watching the News when I gave him mine.

"Are you sure?" he asked.

"The test looks for a special hormone only present in pregnant women, so based on the science it should be impossible to get a false positive once, let alone twice." I told him, rather convincingly.

We were both stunned as the full reality of a new life joining our consciousness, hit us.

On February 16 1998, I met with my doctor, who confirmed what we already knew. I was secretly afraid because I had suffered three miscarriages in the past. The doctors had told me I am what they call an "habitual aborter." This means that if my body determines that my environment is too hostile or stressed to produce a baby, it gets rid it. I had been told just that last year, after the separation with James, that I would probably never be able to carry my own child.

The day I was told that there was not much of a chance for me to have a child, I waited until I got home to break into tears and weep for the child, a piece of me, that I would never hold in my arms. I prayed, and begged the heavens that night that if I could have my own child one day, I would be forever grateful and indebted to them. I accepted then that it would most likely never happen and that if it did, it would be nothing short of a miracle.

As fate would have it, I returned to work the day following my pregnancy confirmation visit with the doctor, to find out that the company I was working for was in big tax trouble. It was also discovered, by management, that the company was stealing earnings from the employees, myself included; 50% of the staff, about 25 people, either quit or got fired that day.

I returned home worried about my job security and the fact that I was now pregnant. I was upset but decided I should relax and hope for the best. I began to unload the dishwasher, thinking about what we would have for dinner, and found myself frozen, as excruciating pain radiated out from my stomach. James arrived home an hour later to find me propped on the couch with my feet up. He could tell from my puffy face I had been crying.

"Paula, what's wrong?" he asked, anxiously.

I told him about the company, the employees leaving, and the horrible pain in my stomach that had started when I got home from work. He became afraid for me then and insisted we should go to the hospital and make sure that the baby was fine.

We were informed by the hospital doctor that I was nearly three months pregnant, not a couple weeks, as we had thought. He also told us if we wanted to keep this baby that I should quit my job and spend the next two to three months confined to bed rest. I was not too happy to learn this, as I have always enjoyed an active lifestyle, but a healthy baby is far more important than any activity or bank balance, so I agreed to leave my job and do my best to rest. James thought it would be a good idea for us to relocate to the town he worked in because to stay in our present residence would mean wasting hundreds of dollars a month in fuel costs commuting three hours a day, all through the winter .

"That's a great idea," I said. "Maybe we'll be able to find a place in the country."

We moved, a month later, to our first house. A quiet,

country, two-bedroom home on acreage in the foothills of the Cascade Mountains, outside the city of Vernon. The doctors had told me if the baby made it five months in-utero, the chances of spontaneously aborting were small and even if that happened, the technology available now would make it probable the baby would survive. I spent my time reading and doing housework at a snail's pace, so I did not upset my oversensitive body.

By the time the five-and-a-half-month mark rolled by, the symptoms that had hindered me during the early months had all but disappeared, and I was feeling much better. For the first time I allowed my self to start falling in love with the little child I was carrying inside me, instead of living with the probability and fear of loss. I took walks on the edge of the wilderness we lived in and felt renewed in my connection to life, the seasons, and the cycles. I felt this moment was paramount in my evolution; this beautiful, tangible transformation from young woman to mother.

We discovered by the end of the summer that there was an ant colony or two living beneath the cottage, and that they would have to be exterminated. For health reasons the pest control officer told us that I would have to leave the house for no less than 48 hours. I called my mother and made arrangements with her to stay for three nights, just to be extra sure the fumes would be gone when I returned.

I made the three hour journey south to my mother's house in Penticton, a few days later. The weather was unrelentingly hot and humid, even for August, and the bus' air conditioning seemed nonexistent, compared to the superior heat of Mother Nature. I appeared and felt like I had swallowed a medicine ball and this heat only added to my already somewhat uncomfortable situation. My mother collected me from the depot and we drove to her home, where she had gifts waiting for our unborn baby.

We spent a quiet night talking about the baby and the impending birth. James called from his grandparents' house after dinner to be sure we had arrived and were doing fine. Shortly after nine I decided to go to bed. I felt exhausted, whether from the pregnancy, the journey, or something else, I do not know. I slept like a rock that night and I awoke the next day with the sun shining brightly. Soon after dinner the phone rang, I picked up knowing it was James.

"Hi, Hon," I said.

"Hey, how are you?"

"Good, we went shopping for maternity clothes today."

"That's good..." He paused and the silence hung between us.

"What's wrong?" I asked.

"You're going to have to stay at your mother's for a few more days because the pest control people pretty much destroyed the place. I've spent the last three hours cleaning and its going to take maybe two more days for me to get everything cleaned up in here."

"What do you mean they destroyed the place?" I asked.

"They moved all of our furniture and pictures off the walls, drilled holes all over the house and they never cleaned up the sawdust from drilling, the residue from spraying, or the thousands of dead ants everywhere."

We talked for awhile longer and then James wished the baby and me sweet dreams and a good night and he told me he would call me again, the following evening.

I believe that it was around 11 pm that I fell asleep on the pullout bed in my mother's living room. My vision cleared from a hazy greyness as I came slowly to consciousness. I was standing, very pregnant, wearing only my bed shirt in some sort of tall cylindrical device. I was in a very tranquil state, as if I knew this had to be done. The cylinder was clear, but had a dark framing covering it in places. What the cylinder itself was made of I don't know.

The nature of the tranquilizing effect made me unconcerned about the surroundings and the Beings I saw around me. I know that if I hadn't been sedated, I would probably have touched everything because I am a curious person; perhaps this was one of the reasons why they sedated me. I can imagine that they would not want curious humans running around touching things or pushing buttons on their ships!

It is funny how when you are in their company, even if you are an adult, you sometimes behave in ways that are childish. Maybe this is why they lovingly call us the "Babies of the Universe." Everything I have seen and learnt thus far in my life has led me to believe that, quite possibly, we are the least developed intelligent species in all the cosmos.

I felt my head being pulled gently back; I did not fight the feeling but allowed my head to go back as far as it could. Now my vision was directed to the ceiling of the cylinder I was standing in. I could see a white disk, about the size of a small pie plate, centered in the ceiling. In the center of the circular pie plate was a dark hole. A clear round tube gently eased out of the dark hole and down towards me. With my head stretched back I watched the tube slowly extend towards me. I felt my mouth opening and I knew instinctively that this tube was going to go into my mouth and down my throat. Part of me, deep inside, *was* afraid but it was like the feeling I get at the dentist, no more.

I didn't want to be there, but I knew, somehow, it was inevitable and needed. I felt my mouth stretching wider than it has my whole life. With my head stretched back and my mouth open I was aligned with the tube. I felt it press past my tonsils and go down my throat. I was aware of a very tight, sliding feeling and I could feel myself becoming incredibly tired. My vision became foggy and I must have lost consciousness then.

I awoke still standing in the cylinder with my head pulled back and the tube down deep inside me. My jaw was cramped and hurting and my throat felt dry and tight. I had the feeling of wanting to swallow to relieve the pain in my throat but the thick tube made it an impossibility. I could not reposition myself to be more comfortable or relieve the pressure from my tired and now slightly shaky legs. I was so tired and I felt like I was stuck on a vertical rotisserie, except I wasn't spinning. I became aware of the sliding sensation of the tube beginning to retract from me and I lost consciousness again.

When I awoke, I was laying on the sofa bed in my mothers' living room. I felt really good, like a happy feeling had washed over me and stuck. My first thoughts were that 'they' were here and that everything was fine, then I felt a violent urge to use the washroom. It was that time of dawn when the sky becomes light but the sun has not yet peaked over the mountain. I rolled out of the bed and saw out the window to my right a craft hovering a mere 50 ft above the neighbors' house that was located directly behind my mothers' place.

The craft was larger than the two-story doctor's house it hovered above. It was a classic saucer shape, domed gently along the top, and was metallic or silver in colour. There were brownish vertical lines across the bottom of the ship and I wondered if they were windows. This was new to me because all the ships I had seen to this point were all 'solid' masses, seemingly devoid of windows or doors and seams. There were pink and reddish lights glowing from the circular bottom of the large metallic UFO. I stared for a moment at the magnificent beauty of this craft, so close to me in the growing daylight.

I heard some rustling noises coming from outside, to the

right of the window I was looking through. I stepped closer, looked to the far right and saw three little Grey Beings walking slowly away. I knew then they had waited to make sure I was okay.

It appeared they had taken this extra step because I was pregnant and what I had endured during the night had been hard on my body. In the same way we humans release tranquilized wildlife, these Beings were waiting for their subject to become conscious before they left.

I saw the three little Greys walking away together and they did not look back. I wondered if they knew I was watching them. Was this a gift for me, another glimpse into an unknown civilization? They walked so close to each other that I felt they must be good friends. I thought how lucky I was to be observing this extraterrestrial behavior and interaction. They seemed to be in good spirits, like three shift workers done for the night. I did not see their faces but I sensed happiness, laughter, and their playful, kind souls.

I looked once more at the ship before my screaming bladder interrupted my thoughts. I turned and walked as quickly as I could to the bathroom and on my way I started to realize how sore my throat, chest, head, and neck really were.

I wondered if they lacked waste facilities on their ships because I don't think I had ever contained this much liquid in all my life. My throat was aching terribly and was so dry it felt cracked inside. I knew I needed to get some water as fast as possible for it felt like there was no lubrication the entire length of my esophagus to my stomach and I could not swallow for the pain.

The happy tranquilizing effect had worn off and been replaced with nausea so intense that I could barely finish relieving myself and flush before I started to vomit violently. I threw up over and over and eventually there was nothing left, yet my body continued to convulse and dry-heave for minutes after. I started to cry from the pain as I could barely hold myself above the toilet with my aching and fatigued muscles. The sounds of sickness and my crying must have woken my mother, who knocked on the door.

"Are you alright?"

"No. I'm really sick," I said

"Well I'll put some tea on to settle your stomach," she replied.

I looked into the toilet thinking this would be a really messed up sample to collect: "Oh yes, and here is the vomit from 1999, with trace elements of unknown origin." No, I would let that particular secret go down the drain. What had come out of me looked like bile; it was yellow and transparent but the odd thing about it, other than my body ejecting this until it felt every last drop gone and had left my throat burning and bleeding, was the interesting crystal-like formations suspended in the liquid.

The tiny crystals looked like snowflakes. They sparkled as light reflected from them, but did not sink or dissolve. If I hadn't been in so much pain, I would have scooped up at least one of these, regardless of where it had come from. My throat was bleeding and I spat out blood a few times before the bleeding seemed to slow down. I flushed the toilet, rinsed my mouth with mouthwash, and walked out of the bathroom on shaky legs.

The conversation that ensued with my mother was one that, had I been feeling a little better, I would have avoided all together. The discussion began with her saying that I would be okay because I was months past having morning sickness. I poured some water and drank thirstily, regardless of the stinging pain it caused going down my throat.

"Paula, you are going to make yourself sick again if you drink so much water," Mom said as I downed my second glass. Had I not been in pain, dehydrated, mentally and emotionally exhausted, I would have just agreed with her, instead of saying what I did.

"I'm not sick from being pregnant. I'm sick because they took me again last night and this time they left me standing for hours with a tube stuck down my throat."

"Oh Paula, you were just dreaming," was the response.

"If I was dreaming then why is my throat bleeding and so dry and bruised that I can barely swallow?" I snapped back at her.

"They're spraying the orchards - that could be why your throat is sore this morning."

I stared into her eyes, defiantly tired of this dance I was forced to do.

"When I woke up this morning the first thing I saw was a ship right above the doctor's house. I heard some noise and when I looked to the right of your house I saw three little Greys, walking away, Mom."

She didn't say a word she just looked at me like she couldn't figure something out.

"Aren't you going to say anything?"

"Well if you say that's what you saw, I guess you saw it."

I must have looked unhappy because she added, "What do you want me to say?"

"Nothing, I'm sorry Mom. I'm just feeling really crappy right now, because my throat and my stomach are really hurting."

My mother and I have had a few conversations like this one, over the years. At first she does not know what to think and naturally, as the child, I have always wanted to be reassured, but to be reassured one has to know that what has occurred is common and natural. My mother was never able to give me much comfort; at best all she could offer was her silence. I could not blame her, for in the area of extraterrestrials we were both uneducated and ignorant.

I am relieved, in a way, that my mother chooses to quietly accept these things that have happened to me from time to time. I feel very fortunate, as I have heard stories of others who, after having been taken, or whatever, and naturally being frightened and shaken from such an odd experience, confide in family or trusted friends only to find themselves classified as having some type of serious brain disorder that requires drug therapy and the use of a padded room.

(In 1997, Dawn Marie, one of my best friends from high school, told me what had happened to a friend of ours: John (not his real name) had told some kids at school that he had been abducted by "aliens." He had also told his foster-parents, who decided, after John became upset and afraid of his experiences, to take him to the hospital. The hospital told John that until he admitted to them that he had made up his extraterrestrial abduction experiences, or agreed that he had hallucinated as a result of drug use, they were going to keep him in the psych ward. I don't know what ever happened to John and I don't know how much truth there really was to that story, but it is an odd point that he was having or reporting experiences at the same time I did. I had moved approximately 220 miles north from the Lower Mainland to the Caribou, with my family, leaving behind all of my childhood friends when I was 15. So it is interesting that I would hear, years later, of someone I knew potentially having experiences of an extraterrestrial nature so many miles away, but during the same time I was experiencing my first live contact events.)

I found it a little difficult not to feel worried the day after the tube experience. I was concerned about the baby because I did not know what had been done to me. I wanted to trust them completely but the only thing that kept me from panic was knowing that I had a doctor's appointment scheduled in three days time. Due to my past difficulties I had a checkup nearly every week or two of my pregnancy. The baby seemed fine to me, as I sat with my hands on my belly, feeling it kicking and moving normally. I understood then that we live in a truly mysterious and fantastic universe and my greatest strength and insight as a human would be to place my trust and faith in that which gives and sustains my life. Basically, I became of the mindset that if I should find my days shortened, the thing that would matter most is what I *did* with the days I had. For this reason I should try to appreciate all the gifts and happiness this life has to offer.

I decided to tell James what had happened at my Mom's, as I didn't want to keep things from him. He took the news much as I expected he might. He was concerned that they had potentially harmed the baby. I assured him by saying that since the last event the baby was moving and feeling to me the same as it always had, and that I was sure it was fine. The appointment with our doctor two days later revealed my intuition had been correct. The baby was perfectly healthy and well.

The remainder of the pregnancy was uneventful, as far as anymore extraterrestrial activity was concerned, and our beautiful, healthy son was born into this world. I continued to see craft in the sky at night and they would make me smile. I have now been personally viewing ships, or UFOs, for more than seven years and yet, beyond the odd report, like maybe once a year, I hear next to nothing from our media with regard to all these intelligent Beings whizzing through our airspace.

Cosmic Responsibility

Around the end of March, 2000, shortly after the snow had melted, I awoke one morning in our country cottage to find the bed sheets dirty once again from my muddy feet. I could remember walking across a cold, partially snow-covered field in the dark. My feet were freezing. I looked down and saw they were dirty and bare. I moved stiffly and painfully. I heard a voice reply to my fearful thinking.

"You don't have much farther to go, you're almost there."

My mind seemed to be devoid of any thoughts about why I was out here and what I might have been doing. I was on my way home from wherever I had been but I can't remember seeing anything but the frozen ground. I must have been in an altered state of consciousness, for I never walk along looking at only what is in front of me and the next step I will take, yet here I was, doing exactly that.

I climbed over the small, wooden, pioneer-homestead-style fence that separated our yard from the field and I saw the frozen ground change into the flagstone path that led to our deck. I was acutely aware of the smoother and warmer feeling of the stone.

Somewhere in my mind this confirmed that my feet were nearly frozen solid, as I had feared they were. The flagstone turned to the wooden deck and was even warmer than the rock had been. My feet were blue and swollen. I remember thinking and feeling with great relief, "I'm home now."

A testament to the powerful trancelike state I was in, a

'neat freak' like me walked right into the house and without so much as wiping my feet, I tracked mud across the floor, down the hall, and into the bed with me and James. Whenever one of these sleepwalking events would happen, I would become disappointed in myself for making such a mess, as I was now. I could remember nothing else. I don't know when I left or returned, nor do I know where I had gone but I didn't think that I had been entirely alone out there in the subzero temperature.

James woke up, and as he threw back the blankets to rise he saw the mud and debris that had melted into our bed from my thawing feet. He immediately assumed our fur-ball, Santana, was to blame. I told him that it wasn't the cat's fault, it was mine. I spent the rest of the morning telling him what I could remember and reassuring him that I was fine and felt well, even though, secretly, I was a little worried and felt that it was probably unsafe for me to be sleepwalking out of my house and into the freezing night. I found my feet dirty three times that week but try as I might, I was never able to remember anything other than the cold steps in the night leading back to my house.

I seemed to go through these periods where I would almost forget about the ETs completely because nothing would happen for months and then there would be a brief period of activity that would remind me that this relationship was not over.

I believe they time their visits, astrologically or other wise. It is my uneducated and humble opinion that these great Beings are establishing and maintaining relationships with humans everywhere. They want us to know that they have always been here, with every generation, helping and hoping that we will be guided towards a more liberated and enlightened future. These farther advanced Beings want us to accept and embrace the fact that we share the cosmos with other species or entities.

Some species are more physical, possessing faster vibrational rates and a condensed matter form, so we can easily see them. Others, with higher vibrational frequencies, may appear as sparks of light or prisms of colour to the naked, untrained eye, but with a little practice it becomes easier to see their presences, and their energy encompassing our entire world. All the worlds, dimensions, and levels of existence are bound and connected to each other; for this very reason our species is not permitted to destroy itself or the environment. It is also for this reason that no species will be permitted to have complete control over another.

I was 24 years old and thought that I had come to finally realize my very small role in the order of things. I did not care, or let it bother me any longer, that I could not remember everything from my experiences, for I felt safer than ever knowing I would know exactly what I should. I felt a renewed sense of inspiration and I was completely content to just live my happy life and continue to record and be appreciative of these interesting aspects to our existence.

The next few months, however, were difficult, as James was very depressed and unhappy in his work and my time was devoted entirely to my little son, James and keeping the house. We separated for the final time in May of 2000. I moved into the downtown area of Vernon, to a decent but old one-bedroom apartment with vaulted ceilings, hardwood floors, and a built-in Victorian tub. I lived with in a stone's throw of shopping and the main city park that had a nice track where I spent many morning hours jogging and pushing my son in his all-terrain stroller, much to his enjoyment.

Over the next eight months I would see craft day and night but I did not have any contact with them directly, that I remember. I did have many nonphysical experiences during this time, but I believe these were to reveal more about the nature and the sheer number of entities that exist here with us.

I decided to move to Penticton in March of 2001 because I was too lonely in this city, where I knew no one and had no friends, save for James' family, who would not even acknowledge me with a wave or smile on the street or in the market. I found a great two-bedroom, second-floor apartment with a working fireplace, right across from the park at Skaha Lake in Penticton, and so I moved happily, with no regrets.

I enjoyed living in this wonderful little city; where there was always a lot to do. My son and I spent many days playing at the beach and in the playgrounds, or going to the many festivals and events held here each year. My son made me feel extremely proud and fulfilled. I marveled daily at this little independent chip off the old block. At a year and half he would play fearlessly unaided at the water park: telling me "No Mommy, me do. Me DO!" He rode down the channel that summer, giving me a fright every time he threw himself out of our dinghy to float behind in his life-jacket, holding a rope to keep him with the boat. I saw 'their' lights all the time but my life was quiet, with no contact that I know of. I barely even noticed their absence from my life, as I was having so much fun being a Mom to my fantastic little son.

In April of 2001, almost a year after my separation, I began to date and eventually moved in with someone else. This new person did not appreciate my having worked on a psychic line (he could be mean and humiliating), so I did not bring up my experiences even when he would comment about the light in the sky that he thought followed us sometimes. This person was abusive when he drank and also became violent. I separated from him and he did the whole 'promise to change' thing and so I found myself, in

October of 2002, moving to Edmonton, where he had taken a job, intending to start a new life there.

A powerful testament to the perfection of God, who works miracles in all our lives, it was while living here, 18 floors above the Edmonton city suburb of Callingwood, that I had perhaps the greatest and saddest realization of my life. I spent my days taking the city transit and dropping off résumés. One day I decided to come home early from my job hunting, as the weather was very nasty and I did not want to freeze to death in the hurricane-force winds during the two-block walk to my building from the bus stop.

I arrived home to the top floor apartment and put some water on for tea, to warm me up a bit. I turned on the TV and I was surfing through the cable channels when I saw a W5 report that caught my eye. I ended up sitting down with my tea, riveted to a story about the how the head microbiologist in charge of testing and approving new drugs and foods for our F.D.A. had been fired after 25 years of excellent service, because of his refusal to endorse the use of a new growth hormone and antibiotic onetime implant for our meat industry.

By the time the show ended, I had tears in my eyes, as this scientist had said that the repercussions from having this introduced into our meat market would be sterility in children who are raised on this food. He also warned that microbial bacteria would cross from our meat into us and that this could skyrocket cancer rates as much as 10,000%, as well as bring a whole new host of problems to our already bombarded healthcare systems.

I changed the station and the next show I found was a program about UFOs that was nearly over. I saw a researcher say that the reason Ufology has been unable to move forward is because the people who are experiencing contact are too afraid to tell their stories, as society has the tendency to humiliate and ridicule experiencers, and so the definitive reports they have to study are mostly decades old. He said that until more people come forward with what they know, nothing will change.

I felt selfish and guilty after hearing this, for my experiences had been secrets that I told to almost no one. I cried, then, for the brutal reality of our lives. Society and the ignorance of others were winning, they were succeeding and keeping me ever so quiet and in fear, for years. A small voice asked a question in my mind: "Paula, how would you feel if you died tomorrow?"

I thought about it and realized that I had rationalized it all in my mind these last few years - that I was just an observer and that there was no reason for me to tell anyone. Even more so, I believed that there were others probably far more advanced and intelligent than I who were going to change humanity's narrow perception of the universe, and so sometime in the future people like me would be accepted and not thought of as crazy or different.

The voice asked again: "But what about you, how will you feel if that does not happen before you die?"

I cried for many minutes as the memories of all my experiences flooded into my head. I had been so sad, alone, and afraid at times, and yet I kept going, believing it would all make sense and be for a reason some day in the future. I cried for those who must have endured this alone, like I had, and I lost respect for our leaders who were appearing more and more to care about nothing other than themselves. I realized I do care, about everyone, regardless of race, religion, or lifestyle. I imagined that if I did die suddenly, all that would be left of me and my experiences would be a few boxes of papers and writing, and my journals. If no one read these, no one ever know about all I had seen and endured. Everything would have been for nothing, and I was a little peeved about this.

I decided I must write down an account of all the undeniably extraterrestrial things I had seen. If I was to die before anything should change, at the very least I might leave behind a rather organized and concise report of my observations and experiences. I realized because I had seen and experienced what I had, that I now had a larger responsibility to others. If there are others out there suffering because of a lack of acceptance and information, then I was now, in a small way, responsible for their continued suffering. I was becoming that which I despised, one who keeps the truth and knowledge from others, thereby prolonging needless pain. Now I was angered and I vowed to myself that it was better to stand or even die for such a good cause, than to fearfully live in hiding from others too ignorant to want or desire the truth.

A few days later, I was moving back to Penticton, BC. The man I was dating drank everyday of my six-week stay and was as violent and mean as ever. I thought life was too short and fantastic to put up with being treated like this and so I packed one day and left, without looking back. I found a nice two-bedroom apartment downtown and a part-time job catering at the hotel, until I could find something better.

I eventually got a full-time job at a call centre and I started to date a nice man who had admitted to me that he had wanted to date me since we had first met, nearly two years before. I told this new man in my life everything about me, as I thought that if he wanted to be with me, he would have to know about and accept the odd things that happened to me from time to time. I was not going to run or hide anymore. I wasn't exactly going to shout from the rooftops either; I just wanted to be honest and truly accepted for all that I am.

Sometime around the end of April, 2004, I sent an e-mail to the Mutual UFO Network, or MUFON, telling them that I had experienced numerous sightings and some contact with extraterrestrials but that I had never previously talked to anyone about what I have seen. MUFON did not answer my letter but forwarded it to a psychiatrist in Colorado, who apparently specializes in abduction cases. This lady seemed nice, until she found out I was Canadian; she said it would be next to impossible for me to drive to her office in Colorado for the many visits she said I would need. After receiving an e-mail from her explaining this, I never heard from her again.

I was very sad that the biggest, most well known UFO research network on our planet had shuffled me off to a psychiatrist. When I wasn't convenient enough to study I was forgotten about. I then knew why so many witnesses don't come forward, for no-one would believe them anyway. Everyone is so caught up spending years to disprove genuine experiences that they miss the truth when it stares them in the face. I decided not to let this get me down. I half expected this type of treatment and besides, this was the first time I had ever tried to contact anyone; maybe the next time would be better. I was in no rush to be disappointed again, so I continued to write down my experiences, in private.

On May 28, 2004, I woke up from a dream in which someone (no body, no face, just a voice) woke me up in my bed to tell me something. The voice told me that the females of our species will continue to grow in power over the next two hundred years. The voice said that Time as we know it is about to end. It said that once before in our history, about 60,000 years ago, we had this same opportunity, but we would not accept it. "You have to reach for it," the voice told me; "we can bring it to you but you have to go after it and reach for it." Then the voice said: "We will work together in the future." I don't think he meant (little insignificant) me, I think he meant all humans and other species will be part of a larger community in the future.

As if I were in my astral body, my consciousness was taken out to our living room, where my turquoise binder, in which I wrote of these experiences, lay on the coffee table. Some unseen force opened my binder and the pages flipped to where I had written a small passage I felt compelled to write down: "All of creation is equal. We all come from the same. Where we begin, where we finish, is one. The source is the path to freedom."

The unseen Being said: "It is this way."

I woke up lying in my bed, just as I had been when the unseen Being had woken me. I waited for a second to make sure I was really awake and then I went out to the living room and flipped through my binder and read the passage again. I wished that I had been able to see who had said these things to me and I wondered why they would tell me all this. I felt happy, though, to have had the experience and I was greatly inspired, and still am, to work hard and do my best, regardless of what others may say or think.

Not many days had passed from my strange waking dream when I awoke on the morning of June 2, 2004, from another notable dream. As a hazy greyness cleared, I came to consciousness, I was standing outside and I saw a Grey Being who seemed to be at least 5 ft tall, struggling with a human man. The human was shirtless, wearing jeans and had dark hair. The dark-haired man appeared to be no older than his early thirties, if that, and was trying to get away from the Grey who had grasped his left arm and was trying to take him somewhere. The man was very terrified and I felt sorry for him being so scared.

"Don't worry," I said "he won't hurt you, he just wants

you to go with him."

Well, that morning, after the dream with the tall Grey, I had the biggest smile on my face. Here I was, a full eleven years since first contact, and I had not been afraid when I saw the Grey but I knew I was there to help him; by helping to reassure the human that he would be okay. I felt happy with myself that I had come this far and now could be of some assistance to these amazing Beings that I had initially been so afraid of.

I knew then that this was the point of repeated contact: to build, develop, and maintain a positive relationship between us. I thought about the dream for days but, try as I might, I could not recognize the man, so I don't think I knew him. I had first thought that maybe we were acquainted, which was why they had called me to help, so this man would see a familiar face and not be afraid. Maybe I was just a familiar *human* face, and I hope that this man is alright and not too traumatized by his experience.

I continued to see the craft during the day and at night, all summer long. I would say a hello to them telepathically every time I noticed them. I was a little sad because I did not have anymore direct contact, that I knew of, but I was contented by the memory of helping the Grey and I was sure that as the contact now had been a part of my life for the last decade, I knew it would most likely continue.

July 29, 2004 was a hot, sunny day. I decided to get out of the heat for a bit and went and sat in the coolness of our tiled living room and turned on the TV. As I surfed through the available cable channels, I came across a popular paranormal show. The episode I saw that day, as fate would have it, was about UFO researchers and their search for proof of extraterrestrials.

They did a large segment on one Canadian ufologist who

has dedicated a lot of his life to this often thankless and ridiculed subject. The ufologist had his contact information posted on the screen at the end of the program, so that other experiencers of extraterrestrial phenomena might get in touch with him. I thought this was too coincidental, and so I sent the gentleman an e-mail. He wrote back right away, and he seemed genuinely happy that I had contacted him. He seemed nice, and intelligent, and I felt at ease after reading the long e-mail he had sent me. He wanted me to relay some of my experiences to him and I did, starting at the beginning, with the experience I remembered with the Golden Being. In the following two weeks I would send him my first three experiences, via e-mail. He had told me to send all my experiences, that he would read them and then tell me what he thought. After sending only three, I was tired of typing and as I hadn't planned on writing an entire book just for him, I asked him to tell me what he thought of my first three major experiences.

He told me that he believed my experiences were memory implants that the ETs had implanted me with "nice" memories, so that they could hide the evil truth. I thought this suggestion was a little strange, as all my memories certainly weren't rosy. When I said that I did not think my experiences had been only implanted false memories, he told me that 99% of all abduction cases reported being raped or being forced to participate in orgies. Therefore, he surmised, if I was a real abductee, I would have been raped by ETs as well, like all the others had (he said I would probably find the out "the truth" under hypnosis).

I never spoke to him again and I did not bother telling him what I thought about his misinformed beliefs. Interesting that someone can make an assumption like that when they have never even seen a ship, let alone one of these Beings.

I was depressed for months after my contact with this disillusioned 'professional' and I certainly did not want to talk to anyone else for a while, if ever. Every time I went to work on my true account of experiences, I would begin to cry. I wanted to believe there were serious non-biased intellects out there, researching and working on this stuff, but I had no evidence. I put my book away, as it had become a too painful a reminder of how alone I really was.

On December 29, 2004, I experienced more projection imagery from the extraterrestrials as I was falling asleep. My eyes could not have been closed for more than a couple minutes when my vision cleared and I saw what looked like some kind of light, sparkling rain appear in the blackness, in front of my eyes. The sparkles of light that looked almost exactly like rain materialized in a contained space in front of me. I felt adrenalized and excited. I opened my eyes.

The sparkling rain was still there, about three feet in front of me and about four feet higher than our bed. The twinkling light was predominantly gold, with white flashes. After a few seconds, the 'rain' cleared and I saw the face and head of a new species of Being. This Being was looking directly at me. I felt in awe of this amazing manipulation of light and matter. I felt safe and remarkably calm in my bed. I stared up and could see that this Being was wearing some sort of spacesuit.

The Beings' head was round and he had large, dark-coloured eyes but that is where the resemblance to any other Being I have ever seen ends. Its skin-covering was white, sparkling star-shine white, with a light green glow in places. The nature of this White Being's facial features leads me to believe that it was wearing a protective suit of some kind. I could easily see the difference between the dark-coloured lenses covering this Being's eyes and those of other ETs' eyes. They were solid black and did not blink, and I felt I was looking into some type of sunglasses, and that the real eyes were behind this dark, protective cover.

There were three vents on either side of the White Being's face, in the area that should have contained a nose and a mouth. The vents were staggered vertically and the first one was located on either side, slightly higher than where you would expect to find a nose. The second vent was located about an inch below and to the right of the first. The third and final vent was an inch below the second but more in line with the first.

I thought the Being looked quite striking in its sparkling white spacesuit, with black eye lenses and black vent covers. I sensed kind thoughts from this Being and that it simply wanted me to observe what it looked like and record this information for future reference. I lay there, looking up at this amazing, silent Being, and I felt a connection to this entity and the others I had seen. I remembered then how we are all on different levels of learning and evolution and yet we are one entire family.

Over the next few months, two more new species projected themselves to me. Had my journals that I started at this time not been stolen in the Spring of 2006 (in what seemed like a very targeted attack on our vehicle just hours before leaving for a short break – my journals, camera gear, a few incidentals, and all our clothes were taken, but a wallet with $700 in was left behind), I would be able to tell you the exact dates. Oh well, all is for a reason. The following projections started just like the first, with a feeling of great energy; I would see the rain like mirage appear and it would clear and reveal what looked like an entirely new physical presence.

I saw one Great Being who must have been quite tall. It looked almost insect-like. It appeared to have a hard skin, or plating, on its dark brown body, and it stood on two legs. It reminded me a little of a grasshopper, for its head and body structure was very similar. I saw this Being was in a dark room and I think he was on another planet, or in a ship somewhere, as the room he was in was dark but had much technological equipment that I did not recognize. This Being wanted me to see it and to know that it was not something to fear. I liked the gentle nature of this Big Brown insect-like Being.

The next Being I saw had golden-coloured skin, large brown eyes, and a large head but this Being had some sort of tentacle-like appendages on his face where his mouth and nose should have been. He could move the appendages and it pulled them back to one side so I could see his proud profile. I was given the sense that he was a great leader of his race and that he had seen many military battles in his time. I felt that he was a general of some type, for he gave me the image of his race as a vast army and that he was a respected commander.

I was amazed and in awe of this uniquely beautiful and powerful Being. I could sense he was a great soul, a noble and honorable Being, and I felt lucky and happy to have the opportunity to be contacted by him. He also sent me the influence that he did not want me to be afraid; I was just to see the truth and remember him. I know they must be smiling, wherever these Great Beings are, for they must know it would be my destiny to write about them.

Shortly before I finished this record of my strange encounters, I learned of the death of a greatly courageous and noble man. I first heard about this scientist/ex-Navy man on a pirated video that was filmed at a MUFON conference I believe took place in 1991 or 1992. This man made such outrageous claims that even the open-minded people who attended this conference were given, at times, to loud outbursts of disapproval or disbelief. The man told the audience that he did not care if they believed him, only that he had to tell people about these things because everyone "deserve[d] to know the truth." By that time, everyone who had worked with him on top secret projects was now dead.

This man's friends and coworkers had been killed for what they knew because certain sub-humans could not have the truth about the ET/human involvement leak out to the public. We all know that if scientists start making claims, we are apt to believe them. This man feared for his life, and rightly so, because he is now dead too, apparently killed by certain 'authorities' in 2002.

This news depresses the heck out of me. I think, what the hell is wrong with this world? At times it truly seems as if we are a race of idiots run by morons. No offence to those who are not idiots or morons (you know who you are); as for those who are, wake up and help make this world what you would like it to be for you and your children. When will we open our eyes and stand united against these injustices carried out against our people and our Earth? I will forever honor the spirit of this man as the hero he is. His loyalty to all of us, as a family that deserves the truth, killed him. I know he was not the first to be taken out in this way, but it is my sincere hope he has been one of the last.

Hearing this brave man's story has not made my job any easier, but I refuse to give in to any form of fear. Some may think that they have control, but we all know intrinsically who has the last laugh. Killing a few people who spout the truth will not stop the truth; because it *is* the truth, and no matter how much time passes, it will always be the truth, right before your eyes.

The Next Stage

In early October of 2005 my fiancée and I took many trips up into the hills that surround our beautiful Okanagan Valley, looking for fallen trees to cut for firewood. On our way home, one of these nights, shortly after the sun had set, as we came down off the mountain with the view of Okanagan Lake in front of us, we saw two unidentified lights in the sky. We pulled over to the side of the gravel road. Armed with my Sony Handi Cam (a Christmas gift from my loving and supportive partner) for exactly this reason, I hit record and let the tape roll.

We watched intently as the two lights, independent of each other, both gained altitude coming up out of Summerland, across the lake. Once the lights had reached 500-600 ft, they began to fly slowly south, towards Penticton. They were very bright and looked like two white, glowing balls. We could not make out the exact size or shape of the crafts and there were no other flashing lights. We were higher than they were and on the opposite side of the lake, on the mountain, as we were parked with a good view of the valley below.

After I had filmed the two white orbs for a few minutes, I suggested that we drive back to town along the now defunct Kettle Valley Railroad (KVR) so that I might be able to tape more of the lights, and I thought we might be able to get closer to them if we followed the track that wound its way along the mountain, above the lake, to Penticton. I stopped taping and we drove quickly to the beginning of the KVR. When we arrived at the trail, not even three minutes from when we had left our parking spot, there was no sign of the mysterious lights. We could see for miles up and down the valley, but the lights seemed to have disappeared. I was a little let down that the lights had vanished so suddenly but I was happy to have captured what I did.

Even though the tape I got was not spectacular proof, I was honored just the same, as this was the first time I had captured their lights on video and at a distance that you could clearly see that the strange white orbs were not planes. I decided shortly after that night that I was going to go back to school. I did not care if it took me the rest of my life, I would rather be working towards truth and knowledge than existing in ignorance. I thought that if society wants to say I am mad because of these things I have seen and experienced, at least I will be a mad scientist! I liked this romantic idea of myself as some strange outcast working on my science and proof of intelligent entities, and I thought, "What could be better?"

I watched their lights in the sky with new interest and I wondered if they had intended to lead me back to school. I think so. I decided I'd better do some upgrading, so I can try to have marks good enough even for medical school, if I want to go that route. I always wanted to be a doctor but I was steered away by unsympathetic parents. In January of 2006, I was pleased to find out that since I never graduated with a diploma that I was eligible for free funding from our government to take all the upgrading I wanted. I believed this was a sign that I was destined to go back to school and that the blessings of the heavens are with me.

I was still seeing ET craft all the time, although mostly at night, and I wondered who else in my area might be in contact with them, too. They seemed to be so busy, zipping here and there, but I never heard anything. There were no reports of abductions, or even sightings, in our area. I was reminded of how alone and scared I had felt when my experiences began and I realized that there probably are experiencers here, but they are too afraid to come forward, like I was. I knew it was time to finish my story, which had sat for nearly a year after I became too depressed from reaching out to the wrong sources.

I was worried and scared about finishing it because I knew it was going to blow the lid off of my quiet, anonymous life, but I also knew I had to finish this story, for myself and the others like me. I prayed, as I have the tendency to do now every time I am overwhelmed and unsure. I prayed for understanding and to know that I was doing the right thing.

Sitting in our living room, all alone that day of realization, a flash of light made the whole room become brighter. I felt at once a sense of peace and warmth come over me. I then saw a man descend through our ceiling but he stopped before his sandal-clad feet reached the floor. He had white hair on his balding head and a white beard. He was dressed in wine-coloured robes and his right arm was outstretched; he held a very large, open, leather-bound book in his hand. His left arm was lifted as if heralding the heavens. I had never seen a vision such as this while awake but I was not afraid. I remembered something a beautiful channel I had the good fortune to meet one day had told me: "If you ever see a presence, ask them to identify themselves and if they won't, then you tell them to go away."

"Who are you?" I asked the robed man

"I am Ezekiel," he said, "I came to tell you, are not alone. This has been done before."

I saw a vision of many noble souls who have worked many lonely years and dedicated their lives to bring truth and knowledge to mankind. I was given the influence not to worry about what others should say or think. I have always been somewhat of a loner and a recluse; I'd rather camp in the hills or read a new book than party at the bars, and this seems to bother some people. The man in the vision told me it is okay to turn away and to claim my life for me. He told me again that this was done before, and then he was gone.

When he told me his name, it seemed vaguely familiar to me. I thought it might be the name of an angel. He did appear to be from up high and his feet never touched the ground. I went to my computer and I Googled his name. What I read brought tears to my eyes and I felt a great sense of release and relief wash over me.

Ezekiel was the first person to write about abduction and ETs and his account is recorded in the Bible. I was amazed to see that his visions from God and the following abduction experiences began shortly after his 30th birthday. I cried again, for my 30th birthday was a just a couple months away. I felt the heavens were trying to allay my fears, as my biggest concern had been: "This has never been done before, so why, God, should I be among the first to bring this to people? I am just a girl and no one of consequence."

My tears were for happiness that God did hear my prayers and that the heavens really did know how hard it can be down here. I was very thankful to have been told I am not alone and that this was done before. I felt a renewed sense of determination and I felt peace with myself and whatever the future would bring. I knew then whatever would happen would be okay, and that our angels are always watching out for us and wanting us to do our best, without fear.

Late in May, 2006, my fiancée decided it would be nice to take the family fishing on his day off. We packed some snacks and the kids into our 4x4 and we headed northeast out of Penticton, up into the subalpine, to Greyback Lake. We had a great day fishing and we caught 14 trout. We headed for home just after the sun had set around 10 pm that night.

As we roared along the gravel logging road on our way home, I noticed a bright white light keeping pace beside us just above the tree line. I had the feeling that I needed to get my camera ready and to make sure I had some tapes. I agreed with the thought in my mind and determined that I would go buy some new tapes the following day. No one else noticed the light and so I made no mention of it, but I determined to get myself ready.

After seeing the light so close to us and the fact that my story was almost done led me to go online and see if I could find any support groups, or just groups with people like me, to talk to. I found the Alien-UFOs forum and I joined. I posted an excerpt from Chapter 2 "The Juvenile" there and I was contacted by a nice researcher from the UK, who was interested in hearing about my experiences. He sent me some really informative reports and I sent him some stills from my video, last Fall, of the two white orbs. For the first time I was feeling truly accepted, sharing information with others who were not biased but like me, just wanting to know more. I was contacted by a few other groups and for the first time in my life I know what it feels like not to be alone with this subject, but to be part of a larger, supportive, and understanding community.

On July 1, 2006, we took the kids to see the Canada Day fireworks and as we were headed home I noticed a light, low and bright in the sky by our house. The sun had set but there were no stars in the clear sky yet, just this light; too low and bright. After we put the kids to bed, we went out to the deck and the light was still there so I grabbed my Handi

Cam to take a closer look.

When I zoomed in on the light it appeared to be spinning very fast and pulsating the most beautiful flashes of colour. It was unlike anything I had ever seen. I taped it for about twenty minutes until it disappeared, and then I went and reported it to UFOs Northwest.

I sent them a DV clip and a few stills. I felt this was a beautiful gift of proof from the heavens as the tape was amazing. I cried that night, with thanks for receiving the opportunity to capture such an image on film.

The following evening I saw the light again, right around 10:00 pm. When I looked through my camera it appeared to be farther away, as it was nowhere near as impressive in movement or colour as the night before. I thought I'd come out again in an hour, at 11:00, and see if it was any closer. The object was still there, but as I zoomed in, it looked like more objects had appeared around the central, greatly illuminated object. I almost could not believe what I was seeing.

The next few minutes were perhaps the most exciting of my life. I began to shake slightly, as I was taping, alone, on the deck. I ran into the house and called for my fiancée and his friend to come and see. I showed them the star and told them to watch as I zoomed in. They became at once afraid and awestruck, for at times there seemed to be as many as 10 objects in the frame. There was a central object that was the brightest and the only one visible with the naked eye, and then there were all these 'orbs' interacting with it.

I reported the sighting and I sent about 20 stills of the multiple objects to UFOs Northwest. I could not believe my luck; it was like the heavens were gifting me with this beautiful footage so that I could add some really good pictures to my book, and also share this amazing video with others. I could not believe what I had taped, for there are no words to describe that which is so foreign to us; all you can do is watch and feel your mind go blank as you have no idea what they are doing or what they are.

While looking over the tape of the multiple objects interacting, in the early hours of July 3, I noticed some very interesting things. When you watch the tape frame by frame, you can see what seem to be objects zipping in and out of the picture. The most amazing discovery was made by my fiancée. He remarked, while viewing a still: "Hey doesn't this look like a face?" I zoomed in on the picture and was awestruck.

There are clearly faces there, not just one but many, as if this were some holographic movie show for interstellar travelers. One of the images appears to be a male human face looking at a projector reel, like from a cinema. I have come to call this, my favourite image, the "Film Man."

Some of the stills appeared to show different species (possibly) and as I had no ability, then, to have this safely analyzed, I became afraid for what might be contained on this tape and I made a decision not to release it, lest it be taken the wrong way by others with less understanding. Since then, of course, things have changed and the footage has been professionally assessed and verified as 'authentic' UFO/ET evidence.

We stand upon the threshold of a glorious future. These Beings are greatly advanced; if they had wanted to destroy us they would have done it long ago. (Fortunately we are they only ones destroying things, like toddlers having a tantrum.) We have nothing to fear from them, as they answer to the same higher authority we all do. GOD. I have been on this planet now for 30 years and two months. During my time here I have seen ghosts of animals and people, extraterrestrials, and angels. I have worked as a psychic, moved things with my mind, and flown in my astral body. It is our love that binds us to all, and we *are* capable of processing vast amounts of energy and information. All of creation is a family. What part will you play?

I know there are those who will scoff at my account of extraterrestrial phenomena. It is told by an average woman but if my story liberates even one other to share his or her long-held-secret account of contact, then I have accomplished my goal. Regardless, now I can continue my education and research, knowing that I have left a record of my strange days here.

Look forward, my beautiful human family, with a smile in your heart, for there is much this life can reveal to us, should we find ourselves willing to accept it.

Light and love to you all.

Paula

Paranormal Research and Eyewitness Testimony

www.eccenova.com

The Face of Our Future?
Extraterrestrial Snapshots

The best stills from the July 2006 UFO footage
taken by Paula Thorneycroft

Colour supplement to
Eye to the Sky

ISBN 978-0-9780981-4-8

Printed in the United States
62535LVS00001B/10-27

9 780978 098155